Walking With God

Exploring Creation, Fall of Man, Laws, and Faith

Terry J. Goble

Walking With God: Exploring Creation, Fall of Man, Laws, and
Faith/Terry J. Goble
1st Edition 2025
(Paperback) ISBN-13: 978-1-966043-00-3
(eBook) ISBN-13: 978-1-966043-01-0

Library of Congress Control Number: 2025902831

DEDICATION

I dedicate this book to current and future generations of Christians hungry and thirsty for knowledge and understanding of our Heavenly Father and seek a deeper understanding of God's love for all His children.

Table of Contents

Acknowledgments

I thank the Father Yahweh (YHWH) (referred to in this book as "God" or "Lord"), our Lord and Savior Jesus Christ (Yeshua Hamashiach), and the Holy Spirit (Ruach Hakodesh) for guidance during this entire process. The endeavor to write this first book of many is through obedience to the Holy Spirit's voice and guidance.

I thank my faithful wife and three children for fully supporting me while writing my first book of many. They have been more than cheerleaders; they have been supportive and understanding, and I am forever grateful.

Thank you to my School of the Holy Spirit Church family and our overseer, Thierry Nakoa, for all the support, encouragement, and push to endure through all obstacles. I pray that all those in our scribal and other classes/courses will significantly impact the world.

Thank you to all of my brothers and sisters in Christ for their encouragement along the way. May we all endure to the end, finishing the race without relenting.

Endorsements

Terry J. Goble's Walking With God: Exploring Creation, Fall of Man, Laws, and Faith is a masterful guide for Christians seeking a deeper understanding of their faith. With profound insights into foundational truths from the Torah to the New Testament, this book presents the Bible as a living, layered text that continually reveals God's purpose for His people. Terry skillfully connects the timeless principles of God's Word—such as the significance of Creation, the Fall, and the Ten Commandments—with the modern believer's spiritual journey. His ability to unpack scripture with clarity and depth provides readers with tools to embrace God's Kingdom, strengthen their faith, and grow closer to Him through prayer, repentance, and trust.

What sets this book apart is its balance of scriptural exposition and practical application. Terry draws on the life and teachings of Jesus, the apostles, and the Hebrew scriptures to illustrate how faith is the fuel of God's Kingdom. His exploration of topics such as the Sermon on the Mount, the role of kingship in understanding God's authority, and the transformative power of faith encourages believers to dive into the Word with fresh eyes. Whether you're a seasoned disciple or a new Christian, Walking With God: Exploring Creation, Fall of Man, Laws, and Faith is an inspiring and indispensable resource for growing in your spiritual walk.

Blessings,

Dr. Arvind Ephraim

(MBA, MSS, MTH, DSS, DTH)

Founder, Author, Coach, ordained and Licensed Minister of Jesus Christ

www.healingpowerministry.org

Introduction

Have you been searching for answers with no resolve? Are you tired of searching the internet till the early morning hours looking for answers that seem so simple? Are you aimlessly searching YouTube for deeper understanding and tired of binge-watching, liking, and subscribing to countless channels and social media influencers? Are you tired of reading book after book, including the Bible, unable to make sense of specific concepts and left confused or unsure? Well, this was me many years ago. New believers have many questions that seem relatively simple, but the answers seem unattainable. Many things were not taught in the local church I grew up in. In this book, I intend to guide all believers closer to God

(Yahweh) and Jesus (Yeshua). During my walk with Christ, there were many roadblocks (and sometimes still are). I have broken down fundamental subjects to provide a good foundation for every believer backed by Biblical principles. Each section has some teaching, personal commentary, and practical application (if needed). I seek guidance from the Holy Spirit for this book to help bring believers out of the wilderness. We should not wander around for 40 years when a two-week journey is all that is required.

This book is broken up into applicable sections and sub-sections with related concepts. One can read through it or pick a section of choice. Each concept covered could be further broken down into a book itself (or already has been by other authors). The context of this book is to lay a solid foundation or to help repair any cracks in a believer's existing foundation. I ask that one keep all the essential items and discard what is already understood or is not needed (eat the meat, throw out the bones). I have read books before, and after over 200 pages, only one concept was extracted. I've blended in light-hearted humor with concise, straightforward answers for your enjoyment. God has led me to write this book, the first of many in a series. I pray this book helps those seeking more answers than words in the many books available today. The Holy Spirit purely inspired everything written in this book. I pray the contents of this book will be helpful, not just now, but for years to come.

The teaching of the wise is a fountain of life, turning one from the snares of death. (Proverbs 13:14)

Before we proceed to the book, I am led to include this simple concept regarding Christianity. R. A. Torrey mentions an important concept in "How to Obtain Fullness of Power." All other religions (except Christianity) leave a person striving to do something to gain God's (or, in some religions, many gods) acceptance or approval to achieve everlasting life or some promise. With the death on the cross, Jesus Christ completed it all for every person on this planet. In summary, all other religions are based on what one can do to win or earn salvation. With Christianity, it has already been done. All we must do is rest in Jesus Christ and believe in His death, burial, and resurrection. In the book "How to Obtain Fullness of Power,"

R.A. Torrey states a brief dialogue between a friend and another, "You have a two-letter religion, and I have a four-letter one. Your religion is *"do."* My religion is *"done."* You are trying to rest in what you do. I am resting in what Christ has done."[1] Do not take notice of those teaching that salvation is by works. Salvation is by faith in Jesus Christ and His finished work on the cross. Jesus died while simultaneously taking on all the sins of the world, past, present, and future. We are all saved through Him and can reconnect with God, just like Adam in the Garden of Eden. If you do not have a relationship (or haven't had a steady one) with the Lord Jesus Christ and at any time while reading this book desire one (or to rekindle your existing one), please go to the section labeled "Prayer of Salvation" in the table of contents. Without further ado, let's start with the basics.

---

[1] Torrey, *How to Obtain Fullness of Power.*

CHAPTER 1

In the Beginning

When in doubt, we should always go back to the basics. The Bible's first five books (the Torah) unpack many fundamental ideas for all believers. Breaking down the Torah entirely would take more literature (not just commentary, but its meaning) to unveil everything fully. The most exciting part of studying the Torah (and the Bible) is that every believer will see, understand, and grasp a new revelation during devotion. Imagine the Bible as an onion; there are many layers. Each layer reveals something new and different. Sometimes, the reveal happens every time (or in certain seasons) the Bible is read. This is why many speak of the Bible "speaking" to them. Realistically, that is the unction (special anointing or empowering) of the Holy Spirit inside of every Believer. This section covers the first few chapters of the Bible and explains the accounts of creation (how we got here) and the significance of the fall of man (how we got into this mess). One thing to remember is that if something doesn't make sense in the Bible, that concept is probably covered somewhere in the Torah. Scripture always backs up scripture. Remember, when in doubt, go back to the basics or the foundation of the Bible, the TORAH.

Creation

One thing that is hard for most people is the idea or belief of the creation, otherwise known as Creationism. Creationism as defined by Merriam-Webster is "a doctrine or theory holding that matter, the various forms of life, and the world were all created by God out of nothing and usually in the way described in Genesis."[2] Public schools

---

[2] "Definition of CREATIONISM."

have been teaching Evolution and the Big Bang Theory to children for well over 30 years (when I was in elementary school). This is devastating to Christianity unless taught in the correct context. Creationism is the fundamental basis of what the Bible teaches in the book of Genesis. I won't go into too much details regarding who and why, but there is evidence to support Creationism and there are various books supporting how it matches up against all other claims.

God Spoke Everything into Existence

In the beginning, God created the heavens and the earth. Now the earth was formless and void, and darkness was over the surface of the deep. And the Spirit of God was hovering over the surface of the waters. (Genesis 1:1-2)

God created the heavens and the earth. Oh, how great Thou art. Let us start by explaining what are the heavens. The heavens are everything in the universe, both seen and unseen. Many speak about the different heavens:

- The first heaven is the Earth's atmosphere, which protects us from the vacuum of space and the sun's (and other star's) rays. Without this, we simply wouldn't be here today. Space is a vacuum; nothing is pressurized like a vessel. Our planet's atmosphere is like an unopened soda can. It's pressurized until you break the seal. We wouldn't be able to breathe if the air couldn't stay contained inside the earth's atmosphere. If we could survive in space, there would be no need for astronauts using space suits to breathe; or the International Space Station and other man-made structures to survive in space. Take a plastic sandwich bag, put it over your mouth, and breathe in until it goes flat. That would be your lungs in space or a vacuum.

- The second heaven is where evil resides and everything demonic resides. Technically, this is everywhere in our universe. Look at ancient cultures and civilizations. They worshipped the moon, sun, stars, other planets, etc. How come ancient civilizations knew more about astrology and its connection to Earth than we do? With all our modern technology and knowledge, we do not know what ancient cultures were fluently operating in daily. My belief is the second heaven is in a parallel spiritual realm that mirrors the universe that some mention as the 4th dimension.

- The third heaven is where God and the Angelic/ Heavenly Hosts reside. The third heaven is mentioned in the Bible by people who have visited there or have seen it (reference The Book of Enoch, The Book of Revelation, Daniel Chapter 7, Isaiah Chapter 6, Ezekiel Chapter 1, and Zechariah Chapter 3 just to name a few books). This is somewhere outside of our universe. It is a pure and spiritual dimension that is totally outside of space and time, but can directly interact with the other heavens (but not all the others have access to this one).

Earth should be self-explanatory as the planet we live on. Per the Bible, the Earth was originally formless and void and was covered in darkness. Some translations say waters, some say the deep. What does this mean? The earth was utterly void. How can the world be void? It is hard to conceptualize. Have you ever seen someone draw up something on 3D modeling software or a program to 3D print something? It is nothingness, completely void, just something in a computer program. Another explanation would be television. When it is turned off, there is no picture. When the television is turned on and has reception or a device plugged in (DVD player, satellite receiver box, streaming box, VHS for the old schoolers, etc.), the screen comes alive. At this point, the television is turned off (formless and void) and nothing [physical] can be seen. With the scripture above (Genesis 1:1-2), the earth is nothingness (formless and void) in the spirit realm. The parallels will make sense soon.

The Spirit of God was hovering over the waters (or deep). Who is the Spirit of God? None other than the Holy Spirit, the third person of the Godhead.

And God said, "Let there be light," and there was light. (Genesis 1:3)

Then God said! This first utterance from God was to create light. The light separated itself from the darkness. This is key for us to understand. With God, there is no gray area, just light and darkness (some would say black and white, good and evil, or positive and negative, and so on). It is my belief that light and darkness is the makeup of the second and third heavens (Respective unseen realms and the universe). Think of the original existence of nothingness. Now, light is created and separates the darkness. Light (originating from the higher 3rd heaven) can actually penetrate the darkness, but the darkness can't penetrate the light. It is also my belief that at this time, the angels and heavenly hosts were all created. The fundamental basis of being a Christian is to separate yourself from the darkness and not live in it. Have you ever mixed oil and water and stirred it up? It remains separated. This is how we should be from the darkness! Moving onto another important part of Genesis 1:3 is who is the Word of God?

> *In the beginning was the Word, and the Word was with God, and the Word was God. He was with God in the beginning. Through Him all things were made, and without Him nothing was made that has been made. In Him was life, and that life was the light of men. The Light shines in the darkness, and the darkness has not overcome it. (John 1:1-5)*

Who might the Bible be speaking of now? None other than our Lord and Savior, Jesus Christ of Nazareth. Do you see how the above scripture, John 1:1-5, parallels Genesis 1:3? Jesus was with God in the beginning. He created all things when God spoke them into existence because Jesus is the Word of God. In Jesus is life and He was the Light of men. We can unpack so much in these five verses alone. In summary, the Light will always overpower the Darkness because the Darkness cannot understand the Light. In conclusion, the Light originates from the 3rd heaven, which the Darkness can't understand.

Notice that the trinity is revealed in the first three verses of the Bible. God, the Father (Genesis 1:1), Jesus the Son (the Word of God, Genesis 1:3), and the Holy Spirit (Spirit of God, Genesis 1:2). This is important to see because it is often overlooked. In summary, all three members of the Trinity were involved in creating everything.

Created in the Image of God

On the sixth day, God created all creatures of the earth, including human beings. God created the human race to have dominion over everything on the Earth.

Then God said, "Let Us make man in Our image, after Our likeness, to rule over the fish of the sea and the birds of the air, over the livestock, and over all the earth itself and every creature that crawls upon it." So God created man in His own image; in the image of God He created him; male and female He created them. (Genesis 1:26-27)

When God said, "Let Us," He wasn't talking about an alien race, multi-dimensional beings, or the like; He was stating the Father (God), Son (Jesus, the Word of God), and Holy Spirit created human beings. God commanded it, the Son/Word spoke it, and the Spirit made it. Since we are created in the image of the Godhead (Father, Son, and Holy Spirit), we are created in their likeness. What does that mean for us? Just as God's works spoke everything into existence, our words have creative power.

Life and death are in the power of the tongue, and those who love it will eat its fruit. (Proverbs 18:21)

We need to say good things always. One thing that happens with most people is they can't control their tongue. Jesus even mentions this during one of his teachings regarding the Pharisees.

Jesus called the crowd to Him and said, "Listen and understand. A man is not defiled by what enters his mouth, but by what comes out of it." (Matthew 15:10-11)

People unknowingly speak curses over themselves every day. When we don't speak "love" with each other, we can come from a negative place. If we speak from these negative places with ill motives, they can come back and hurt us. We must speak to and treat others how we would like to be spoken to and treated. Jesus mentions in John 13:35 that everyone will know His disciples by their love for one another. The Lord has recently dealt with me on this one. I would ridicule and say ill things about certain leaders in Christian circles. I don't think that way anymore. If we feel someone is in error, it is best to confront and speak to them directly and pray for them. Praying for and loving everyone, even our enemies, has endless rewards in the kingdom of heaven.

A lot of business professionals, secular people, and the like teach this to get ahead in business. They say to speak affirmations over your life. They say to keep seeking and believing wealth and prosperity will occur. It could, but they are operating in witchcraft because they aren't relying on God! They are relying on themselves and self-creating the reality they want to live in. This is the fruit of death. Why you ask? Well, relying on one's self and one's own will (or soul) power to make things manifest is pure witchcraft. We must one hundred percent rely on God and the Holy Spirit for all things.

Now, the fruit of life is what we will cover later on in this book. The teachings of Jesus show the ways to life and spiritual life. If we operate in witchcraft, that is spiritual death. What is not in this book is the book of Proverbs. Proverbs will also cover these concepts. Read the book of Proverbs with all your senses and listen to what the Holy Spirit reveals to you. It might change each time you read it by something new standing out. Remember, the Bible has to be taken in layers to fully understand its entire contents.

Concluding Thoughts

God created all things and the entire trinity was revealed in the first verses of Genesis. It is important to know where we come from and how we all came into existence. This has been an age-old question, and it is right in the first couple of chapters of the Bible. Almost equally important, what side are we for, the light or the darkness? I'll boldly share simple truth, the Light will always win. The smallest speck of light can illuminate the darkest room or area. Never underestimate the light that is inside of you. All it takes is a spark to light a forest fire.

Practical Application:

We need to be rooted fully in the faith. Our foundation has to be firm in what we believe. If we don't believe it, then our foundation is weak and can break. What happens when it breaks? Well, that allows the enemy to creep in. If your house foundation has a small hole in it, mice and snakes and bugs or worse can creep in. We must maintain our house to keep it clean. The best maintenance man out there is Jesus. His work is always top-notch, and better yet, He works for free! All we must do is know He will show up and believe the work will be done.

- The Godhead (trinity) was revealed in the first three verses of the Bible.
- God (Genesis 1:1),
- Word of God (Jesus, Genesis 1:3), and
- The Spirit of God (Holy Spirit, Genesis 1:2)
- Everything was created from nothingness. God formed and shaped and created everything.
- We are created in the image of the Godhead. There is power in what we say. We should speak wisely and speak out of love for all.

CHAPTER 2

---◆◯◆---

The Fall of Man

One important item often overlooked or not fully understood is the Fall of Man. The whole reason we all live in a fallen world is because of this one event. Let us look at how the world was before this event:

> "'And God looked upon all that He had made, and indeed, it was very good. And there was evening, and there was morning—the sixth day'" (Genesis 1:31).

In the world before the fall, everything that God had made wasn't just good, it was very good. This included all plants, animals, and human life. Everything was perfect according to God's design.

Have you ever built something and then it accidentally gets dropped, or stepped on, or broken? I'm sure this has happened to all of us. So, what happens after it gets dropped, stepped on, or broken? It can be restored close to the original but can't get back to 100% the same as when it was newly created. This is not according to God's original plan, but it is what happened in the Garden of Eden.

Who Really Disobeyed in the Garden?

Not to point fingers at anyone, but it is very important to understand who ultimately caused the event known as the Fall of Man. The background of life in the Garden of Eden is that man was created. That man's name was Adam. Then God brought all the animals to Adam to name them. Then, God felt bad for Adam. God made man a suitable helper to tend in the Garden, woman (See Genesis 2:18-25). We need to back up to before God brought Adam (man) the animals to name.

Then the LORD God took the man and placed him in the Garden of Eden to cultivate and keep it. And the LORD God commanded him, "You may eat freely from every tree of the garden, but you must not eat from the tree of the knowledge of good and evil; for in the day that you eat of it, you will surely die." (Genesis 2:15-17)

Per the previous explanation, Adam was first put in the garden to tend to it. Afterwards, the woman was created, as mentioned earlier. Since Adam was created before woman, he was ultimately given charge over the Garden of Eden. Then what happened when Adam let his guard down?

Now the serpent was more crafty than any beast of the field that the LORD God had made. And he said to the woman, "Did God really say, 'You must not eat from any tree in the garden?' "

The woman answered the serpent, "We may eat the fruit of the trees of the garden, but about the fruit of the tree in the middle of the garden, God has said, 'You must not eat of it or touch it, or you will die.' "

"You will not surely die," the serpent told her. "For God knows that in the day you eat of it, your eyes will be opened and you will be like God, knowing good and evil."

When the woman saw that the tree was good for food and pleasing to the eyes, and that it was desirable for obtaining wisdom, she took the fruit and ate it. She also gave some to her husband who was with her, and he ate it.

And the eyes of both of them were opened, and they knew that they were naked; so they sewed together fig leaves and made coverings for themselves. (Genesis 3:1-7)

The great deception, notice how the serpent used his persuasion to lead the woman astray and twist the words of God. The serpent put doubt of God's words in her innocent mind. Then, the serpent lied by twisting the truth. The serpent knew she wouldn't die physically, but dying spiritually was a different story. Originally, Adam and the woman had a 100% direct connection to God. They were operating at 100% capacity in the spirit. To do that, they did not need to be wise in this world; they were just obedient to God's commandments. Did you catch that? The woman didn't know how to discern the serpent's intentions because she continually lived without fear or manipulation and completely trusted everything (she was naïve).

Notice the woman's initial answer. She said you can't even touch the tree or you will die. If we look above at what God initially originally told Adam in Genesis 2:16-17, He just said that if you eat of it, you shall die. Then there is the serpent. The serpent says that she won't die and that her eyes will open and will be like God. The woman then looked at the tree and her entire perspective changed. Can you remember when this happened to you? Hearing something slightly true or not and your whole perspective on something changed. This is something that the enemy excels in and has been doing since the beginning of time. So, the woman ate from the tree and then gave her husband, Adam, some to eat. Their eyes were opened from that day forward (of what is good and evil). So, who was at fault here? The woman ate from the fruit first, but who was the keeper of the garden? Yes, Adam was at fault. Adam was given a direct commandment from God not to do something, and he disobeyed. What is even more hilarious is that Adam was right there with her during the whole thing. I can imagine Adam saying, "Oh, look at that talking serpent. Just another day in the garden, isn't it honey?" I can imagine Eve rolling her eyes at Adam, saying, "Listen, this serpent sounds pretty intelligent. Can you draw a picture of us talking?" Wouldn't it be just like human beings? The first selfie caused the Fall of Man.

What Happened After Eating the Forbidden Fruit?

The easy answer, humanity fell into sin or spiritual death. Out of every tree in the garden, they ate from that one. Have you ever told your children or remember from childhood, "Don't touch that one thing?" It might have been a special picture, project, fine China, something valuable, etc., and what would happen? We or they would touch it and almost be the first thing done after being told not to. Proportional to our inherent sin nature are some of the natural reactions we have.

Going deeper into what happened is Adam disobeyed God. The disobedience caused sin to enter the equation and ultimately separated Adam and the woman from God. To dwell on how sin entered all of humanity and go on a much-needed tangent, what does the Bible say?

> You shall not bow down to them or worship them; for I, the LORD your God, am a jealous God, visiting the iniquity of the fathers on their children to the third and fourth generations of those who hate Me, but showing loving devotion to a thousand generations of those who love Me and keep My commandments. (Exodus 20:5-6)

Then the LORD passed in front of Moses and called out: "The LORD, the LORD God, is compassionate and gracious, slow to anger, abounding in loving devotion and faithfulness, maintaining loving devotion to a thousand generations, forgiving iniquity, transgression, and sin. Yet He will by no means leave the guilty unpunished; He will visit the iniquity of the fathers on their children and grandchildren to the third and fourth generations." (Exodus 34:6-7)

The scripture from Exodus 20 above is from the second commandment. Basic disobedience of God's commandments will visit through three to four generations. If, and only if, they don't do that iniquity anymore. In Exodus 34 above, Moses just got done interceding for the Jewish people in the wilderness. God mentioned the same thing. If one is guilty of disobedience, that disobedience will be with them for three to four generations. Could it get any worse?

No one of illegitimate birth may enter the assembly of the LORD, nor may any of his descendants, even to the tenth generation. (Deuteronomy 23:2)

An illegitimate child and their bloodline to the tenth generation will be affected. Look at how many single parents or non-married couples are having children. In many countries nowadays, these are called domestic partnerships or similar. No wonder the enemy is trying to break up the traditional family structure. Those born out of wedlock will feel the effects for up to ten generations (or longer if it is a continual cycle). Let's turn away from the physical and look to the spiritual. What if a spiritual child of God becomes uncleaved to Him? If we are not living as a child of God, wouldn't that make us a bastard (or illegitimate) child? Ouch! That might have hurt, but look at scripture and put it together. If we walk in disobedience, as Adam and the woman did, we become separated from God, thus making us illegitimate children. If we continue to walk that way, our descendants will not enter the assembly of the Lord. Luckily, God loves us dearly and will take us back with open arms like the Prodigal Son (see Luke 15:11-32). Okay, so back to the original dialogue of Adam and the woman.

If Adam and the woman were 100% operating in the spirit beforehand, God always knew where they were.

But the LORD God called out to the man, "Where are you?" (Genesis 3:9)

Does one truly believe it was normal for God to call for them in the garden? He is the creator of all, the entire universe. God is omnipresent, omnipotent, and omniscient. God knew where they were, even though He wasn't spiritually connected to them anymore. It was as if God didn't recognize them because of their sin, hence he was asking where they were. Adam and Eve were terrified and was the first time they have ever felt shame.

> "I heard Your voice in the garden," he replied, "and I was afraid because I was naked; so I hid myself."
>
> "Who told you that you were naked?" asked the LORD God. "Have you eaten from the tree of which I commanded you not to eat?" (Genesis 3:10-11)

Busted! Of course, Adam was scared. He didn't know what the repercussions were going to be. Put yourself in Adam's shoes, I remember hiding from my dad before when I was a child. I was scared and was going to hide out as long as possible. Eventually, I had to face my dad and explain what had happened. Likewise, when we are in Adam's situation, we all have to face God and explain ourselves. Adam's response probably sounds oh so familiar.

> *And the man answered, "The woman whom You gave me, she gave me fruit from the tree, and I ate it."*
>
> *Then the LORD God said to the woman, "What is this you have done?"*
>
> *"The serpent deceived me," she replied, "and I ate." (Genesis 3:12-13)*

The woman whom You gave me, she gave it to me and I ate! Come on, Adam! You were the keeper of the garden! I bet God wanted to pull a Homie the Clown from In-Living Color and *THUMP* (hit in the face with a bar of soap in a sock) "God don't play that." In all seriousness, Adam played the blame game. Adam blames the woman and God in the same sentence. Wow! We've all been in that situation, myself included.

Then, the woman fesses up and shares the truth. We need to dwell here for a bit. One sin, one act of disobedience, separated humanity from God until Jesus came. Please don't fall into the trap of "Oh it is just a white/minor lie" or "It is okay, no one is looking" or "No one is around, no one will know." From what I mentioned earlier about the attributes of God, He knows. If we sin or walk in disobedience, we become slaves to that sin or action. Remember from earlier about how sin affects not just us, but our future generations. It is often said that ninety-nine percent obedience is one hundred percent disobedience. Please don't be disobedient and fall short of the glory of God. The great thing about God's grace is that if one unknowingly sins, they will be forgiven as long as they repent and don't do it anymore. Since Jesus' finished work on the cross, we are saved from this forever separation from God.

Speaking of Jesus' finished work on the cross, what did that all do? What happened when Adam and Eve sinned is they handed over their dominion over the earth to Satan. After their disobedience, everyone born after them could not experience the presence of God. Everyone born after them became slaves to sin and were bound to hell when they died. What did God do?

"And I will put enmity (open hostility) Between you and the woman, And between your seed (offspring) and her Seed; He shall [fatally] bruise your head, And you shall [only] bruise His heel."(Genesis 3:15 AMP)

In the above passage, God spoke to the serpent and cursed it. So, what does this all mean?

Hostility will be between the children of the woman (followers of God) and the followers of the serpent (Satan). Jesus is the "He" that shall fatally bruise the serpent's head; yes, this is the first mention of the coming messiah in the Bible. The bruising of His heel is the serpent can only hurt the coming messiah. The serpent couldn't kill him. You see, Jesus gave himself up freely as a sacrifice. Jesus could have said no, but He obeyed God. Through the sacrifice of Himself on the cross, Jesus took back the dominion of humanity to experience God's presence and blessing. Now, heaven is available to us instead of a different section of hell.

Concluding Thoughts

Who would have thought that Adam blamed God and the woman in the garden for the fall? Regardless, the Fall of Man is a significant event. It has led humanity into the position it is and was in. Before Jesus came, everyone in the world was born into a naturally sinful nature. The people of the earth then could not experience God's presence and love. Read the accounts of the people in the Bible in the Old Testament. The people of Israel constantly fell away from God. The utter destruction of Sodom and Gomorrah and the Great Flood was all because of the people's wickedness. God is always faithful and will always give His creation a solution.

Practical Application:

Let us learn not from experience. Let us learn from scripture in the Bible the word of God. Sometimes, it is necessary to go back to the beginning and see what we can find. So much is in the Torah (Genesis, Exodus, Leviticus, Numbers, and Deuteronomy). An intense study of it will uncover many things we might often overlook.

- We need to be obedient to what God (also Jesus and the Holy Spirit) commands us to do otherwise we will fall into sin.
- Once in sin, we are in disobedience and can be separated from the presence of God.
  - This separation can be generational until one comes along that restores that connection with God.
- No matter how little the sin is, it is still sin.
- Remember this: Ninety-nine percent obedience is one hundred percent disobedience!
- Jesus has redeemed us from the curse of sin and death.

CHAPTER 3

God's Laws

The God of Abraham, Isaac, and Jacob isn't just a good God, He is a just God. God is a God of order. He has placed everything "in order" for a reason. He is the creator of all. Why wouldn't God establish rules?

"Worthy are You, our Lord and God, to receive glory and honor and power, for You created all things; by Your will they exist and came to be." *(Revelation 4:11)*

One thing I will get into later is that God is a King, and kings rule through a monarchy. Understanding what kings do and their attributes can help us understand God even more. There are many examples in the Bible about kings and how they rule. The King established all the laws (set decrees) of the land. The king also couldn't revoke the laws set in place.

> *So King Xerxes (Ahasuerus) said to Esther the Queen and Mordecai the Jew, "Behold, I have given Haman's estate to Esther, and he was hanged on the gallows because he attacked the Jews. Now you may write in the king's name as you please regarding the Jews, and seal it with the royal signet ring. For a decree that is written in the name of the king and sealed with the royal signet ring cannot be revoked." (Esther 8:7-8)*

> *He established them forever and ever; He issued a decree that will never pass away. (Psalm 148:6)*

> *In the future, when your son asks, "What is the meaning of the decrees and statutes and ordinances that the LORD our God has commanded you?" then you are to tell him, "We were slaves of Pharaoh in Egypt, but the LORD brought us out of Egypt with a mighty hand. Before our eyes the LORD inflicted great and devastating signs and wonders on Egypt, on Pharaoh, and on all his household. But He brought us out from there to lead us in and give us the land that He had sworn to our fathers. And the LORD commanded us to observe all these statutes and to fear the LORD our God, that we may always be prosperous and preserved, as we are to this day. And if we are careful to observe every one of these commandments before the*

LORD our God, as He has commanded us, then that will be our righteousness." (Deuteronomy 6:20-25)

Therefore, we can always trust in God because He is always trustworthy and faithful to His word. As mentioned in the earlier section (In the Beginning), God created the Heavens and the Earth. This also means that He created everything behind what and how we interact with this physical experience. Let's review some items learned in school, but look at it from a different light.

Physical Laws

Physical Laws is the name I will coin this portion. This comprises everything from math and science that we learn about in school. Do you desire to know the answer to all the big questions of why and how everything interacts the way it does? It was all, per God's design. We have a hard time grasping this concept and want to break down or argue against minute items, which in the end will not make a bit of difference except for the sake of arguing. We live in a digital world where everyone has access to the internet to seek information daily. Whether good or bad, we all rely heavily on it now. Older generations had to memorize everything and knew how to do everything via books, reference tables, pencils, and paper (notice I didn't mention a calculator). Heck, I remember Peter from my junior college. He could do calculus in his head! I'm not picking on Peter; I'm just stating how powerful our minds are at certain things if we rely on them more than electronic devices. God designed us that way. Before I get off on a tangent, let's dive into some science.

Merriam-Webster defines "Science" as:

Knowledge or a system of knowledge covering general truths or the operation of general laws, especially as obtained and tested through scientific methods.

Such knowledge or such a system of knowledge is concerned with the physical world and its phenomena.

A department of systematized knowledge as an object of study.

Something (such as a sport or technique) that may be studied or learned like systematized knowledge.

A system or method of reconciling practical ends with scientific laws.[3]

---

[3] "Definition of SCIENCE."

I hope these definitions reinforce our concept of what science is. Notice how the words "System of Knowledge" and "Systematized Knowledge" are used? This means that over time, many people tested the beliefs of people. Through this testing, items were proven to be found true, false, or a "Theory." The many categories of "Science" include Earth Science, Chemistry, Physics, Statics, Dynamics, Mechanics, Thermodynamics, etc. One way to prove this is gravity. We are taught that gravity on Earth and all other planets (and moons) are at a certain constant force dependent on their overall mass. This means that on Earth, drop a penny and a gallon of water from the same height, they will both hit the ground at the same time. Without taking aerodynamics and other factors into play (i.e. a feather vs bowling ball wouldn't be a good example); the math would get super complicated and wouldn't be an accurate comparison. In short, gravity works the same on every planet, but at different rates. When calculating friction (yes, physics teaches one how to do this), one has to factor in potential (gravity is part of potential energy) and kinetic energy. When figuring out molecular bonds in chemistry, again, a time-proven method is taught in schools.

The truth I want to share is this is all possible because it was all designed to happen this way. If anything was truly possible to happen (and allowed to happen) by man's will or design, everything would be in utter chaos. Look at what happened with the Tower of Babel:

Now the whole world had one language and a common form of speech. And as people journeyed eastward, they found a plain in the land of Shinar and settled there.

And they said to one another, "Come, let us make bricks and bake them thoroughly." So they used brick instead of stone, and tar instead of mortar. "Come," they said, "let us build for ourselves a city with a tower that reaches to the heavens, that we may make a name for ourselves and not be scattered over the face of all the earth."

Then the LORD came down to see the city and the tower that the sons of men were building. And the LORD said, "If they have begun to do this as one people speaking the same language, then nothing they devise will be beyond them. Come, let Us go down and confuse their language, so that they will not understand one another's speech."

So the LORD scattered them from there over the face of all the earth, and they stopped building the city. That is why it is called Babel, for there the LORD confused the language of the whole world, and from that place the LORD scattered them over the face of all the earth. (Genesis 11:1-9)

Were the people building the tower of Babel doing great in their own eyes? Of course, but in God's eyes, they were not. Their pride was getting the best of them. Nowadays, we have people figuratively building their own towers of Babel that aren't glorifying God. It is best mentioned by the Apostle Paul:

"Therefore, my beloved, just as you have always obeyed, not only in my presence, but now even more in my absence, continue to work out your salvation with fear and trembling." (Phillipians 2:12)

Pride is a hideous thing and will lead anyone to ruin. Aside from pride, people want to glorify themselves by having or doing outlandish things. We should always stay humble and reserved in speech and actions.

All this science talk might sound familiar from school, but everything will come full circle soon. In Science, we view everything from our own perspective to understand the world (and universe) better. God has created all, defined all, and knows all; we don't have that capability or capacity. As human beings, we have to work to understand anything by using the scientific method. The scientific method starts with a "Hypothesis."

Merriam-Webster defines Hypothesis as:

An assumption or concession made for the sake of argument.

An interpretation of a practical situation or condition taken as the ground for action.

A tentative assumption made to draw out and test its logical or empirical consequences.

the antecedent clause of a conditional statement.[4]

People who are intellectuals and thinkers can come up with all kinds of hypotheses. When reviewing the definition of Hypothesis, "Interpretation" and "Assumption" are mainly used. When we find something in science that could be that missing link to a law or a new understanding, it simply starts with a thought that has to be proven. Once that thought proves to be valid, it can then become a theory. Theories are used often in science and have almost taken place as a Law because, over time, they haven't been proved wrong.

---

[4] "Definition of HYPOTHESIS."

Merriam-Webster defines "Theory" as:

a plausible or scientifically acceptable general principle or body of principles offered to explain phenomena.

a belief, policy, or procedure proposed or followed as the basis of action.

an ideal or hypothetical set of facts, principles, or circumstances.

a hypothesis assumed for the sake of argument or investigation.

a body of theorems presenting a concise systematic view of a subject.

the general or abstract principles of a body of fact, a science, or an art.

the analysis of a set of facts in their relation to one another.[5]

Without getting super nerdy, theories that have been believed to be true for a long time have been proven wrong. As we keep evolving with technology, more understanding can be applied to better understand the world and universe we live in. In the definition above, the words "Plausible" and "Hypothetical" and "General or Abstract Principles" are used. Theories aren't solid, known, or fully understood, even when believed and used

---

[5] "Definition of THEORY."

for long periods. In the end, Theories are still just Theories. They aren't a known truth or law.

Truth is what all people should rest in. Christians should rest in the Word of God. In the Word is God's promises. Many, many times, science has tried to disprove the Bible. They found Babylon (in modern-day Iraq) in the early 1800s. This was a monumental discovery! For over 2000 years, everyone said Babylon was a mythical place and didn't exist until they excavated it. The land of Ur that Abraham and Sarah came from, no one knew where that was. Look up Sumeria online (also in modern-day Iraq), Ur was part of the Sumerian kingdom[6] which ultimately became part of the Babylonian empire.

Creationism vs Evolution has its arguments. Creationists have valid points, but scientists who believe against creationism state that "Evolution" is merely a theory, not a law. These same scientists also agree that everything has an intelligent design and can't manifest out of thin air[7]. I believe that is the common belief between

---

[6] Mark, "Ur."

[7] Rennie, "15 Answers to Creationist Nonsense."

the two. There is ultimately a creator. Per what is written in the Bible, God created all.

Mathematics

Mathematics is used in science and in almost every part of our lives. In the house you live, math was used to create the foundations, and build the walls and ceilings. Blueprints had to be followed by the builders. Whoever builds computers, automobiles, clothes, bottles, cans, basically anything, they have to use math to design everything to be built. Mathematics is often described as a "Universal Language" because, no matter what language one speaks, mathematics is all the same. Humanity has developed mathematics over time. I bring up mathematics to not give anyone PTSD from school; rather, to give clarity on what has been used to understand what God established at the beginning of time.

On Earth as It Is in Heaven

This section is not to review the lyrics of a Chris McClarney song (even though I really like that one), it is to review the concept of "On Earth as It Is in Heaven." I have to mention that at the time of writing this book, I stumbled across a book by Dan Duval of Bride Ministries in Katy Texas named "Higher Dimensions, Parallel Dimensions, and the Spirit Realm" that explains a lot more than I am mentioning here. This concept is mentioned in the famous prayer that Jesus taught to the disciples:

> So then, this is how you should pray: 'Our Father in heaven, hallowed be Your name. Your kingdom come, Your will be done, on earth as it is in heaven.' (Matthew 6:9-10)

Multiple places in the Bible list or mention God as being the ruler of the heavens and the earth, but is not the only one ruling. As keys are given by the Lord or discovered in the Bible, God is partnering up with those whom He entrusts those keys. Per the words of Jesus again, he mentions to Peter after he proclaimed Jesus as the Christ:

> I will give you the keys (authority) of the kingdom of heaven; and whatever you bind [forbid, declare to be improper and unlawful] on earth will have [already] been bound in heaven, and whatever you loose [permit, declare lawful] on earth will have [already] been loosed in heaven." (Matthew 16:19 AMP)

Look closely at the verbiage: what is bound/loosed on earth shall be bound/loosed in heaven. The only conclusion is that the physical and spiritual realms are tied together (as previously discussed). Dan Duval mentions he believes that during creation, Spiritual templates were created of everything to be created into physical items.[8] This ultimately means that the Spiritual realm is higher than the Physical because the Spiritual created the Physical. I also want to mention that this does not mean that all spiritual beings can create items in the Physical realm. God is the one that can create and did create all things. Given the angle of everything created in the physical started with a spiritual template or was from the spirit, this opens up so many scripture references, like:

> *"Before I formed you in the womb I knew you, and before you were born I set you apart and appointed you as a prophet to the nations."* *(Jeremiah 1:5)*

God knew us before we were born, every one of us! Why? Everything started in the spirit realm before it could be created in the physical. No wonder everyone says God never stops working. With over 8 billion people in the world at the time of writing this book, imagine how many human

---

[8] Duval, *Higher Dimensions, Parallel Dimensions, and the Spirit Realm.*

babies are made or born each day (let alone animals in the wild, on the entire planet) and they are all being created by God. I hate to bring in other topics, but this is why abortion is wrong. Thinking of killing/murdering someone is a sin and is the same as doing it, even if an unborn child, fetus, embryo, or whatever you want to call it, it is still a creation of God. God created the Spiritual and allowed the physical to manifest.

I have heard discussions of people stating that all around us are invisible wars. This can be backed up by the book of Daniel.

> *I lifted up my eyes, and behold, there was a certain man dressed in linen, with a belt of fine gold from Uphaz around his waist. His body was like beryl, his face like the brilliance of lightning, his eyes like flaming torches, his arms and legs like the gleam of polished bronze, and his voice like the sound of a multitude.*
>
> *Only I, Daniel, saw the vision; the men with me did not see it, but a great terror fell upon them, and they ran and hid themselves.*
>
> *So I was left alone, gazing at this great vision. No strength remained in me; my face grew deathly pale, and I was powerless. I heard the sound of his words, and as I listened, I fell into a deep sleep, with my face to the ground. (Daniel 10:5-9)*

WOW! An angel appeared to Daniel, but no one else could see it. If no one else could see it, then how were they afraid and ran away to hide? There was a manifestation of the spiritual in the physical. One other important thing the angel mentions is:

"Do not be afraid, Daniel," he said, "for from the first day that you purposed to understand and to humble yourself before your God, your words were heard, and I have come in response to them. However, the prince of the kingdom of Persia opposed me for twenty-one days. Then Michael, one of the chief princes, came to help me, for I had been left there with the kings of Persia." (Daniel 10:12-13)

Two main points we can pull from these verses:

1. God heard Daniel from Day One. Always remember this: God always hears our prayers.
2. The Prince of Persia resisted the angel until Michael, a chief or arch-angel, was sent to assist.

Let me explain the Prince of Persia. God is a God of order. He establishes laws as we have and are still discussing. Almost everywhere in the Old Testament, there is some pagan god that is over a people (or that a people group worships as their god). Sometimes, there are many (like in Egypt, Greek, Rome, etc.). The point is that people worship who they want to worship and glorify who they want to glorify. God chose the Hebrew people. A remnant people through one man named Abraham became the great nation of Israel. The Prince of Persia was whatever demonic power that opposed God in that particular region of the world. For the context of this section, every country, nation, region, etc. has a power over it depending on what the people worship and glorify. Why do you think God mentions to have no other gods before Him? Also, why shouldn't we build or have idols? That means God is not number one in our lives if something or someone (including ourselves) else is set above Him. Some might see this as a tangent, but just as there are kings, presidents, prime ministers, etc. in the physical, there are also spiritual powers over those regions. Those spiritual powers can affect those in the physical realm. Every city, state, region, country, etc. has a different "feel" about it. Some things are strikingly common, including poverty, violence, thought patterns, speech, etc. People from New York City act and sound different than someone from Chicago, Dallas, Los Angeles, London, Tokyo, and so on. In conclusion, all are being affected differently by spiritual powers.

Spiritual Laws

Spiritual Laws for a new believer might sound peculiar. We are so used to interacting with the physical that we forget about what can't be seen. Faith and Hope fuels everything in the Kingdom of God, while believers operate in Love. For this section, we are going to focus on Love (Faith is covered later) and its importance. People not of God use witchcraft, which is broken down by Derek Prince as intimidation, manipulation, and domination.[9] If we operate in any of those three ways, we aren't doing things in love (which is directly against what Jesus taught). Paul explains the importance of Love in his first letter to the Corinthians:

> If I speak in the tongues of men and of angels but have not love, I am only a ringing gong or a clanging cymbal. If I have the gift of prophecy and can fathom all mysteries and all knowledge, and if I have absolute faith so as to move mountains, but have not love, I am nothing. If I give all I possess to the poor and exult in the surrender of my body, but have not love, I gain nothing. Love is patient, love is kind. It does not envy, it does not boast, it is not proud. It is not rude, it is not self-seeking, it is not easily

---

[9] *Derek Prince.*

angered, it keeps no account of wrongs. Love takes no pleasure in evil, but rejoices in the truth. It bears all things, believes all things, hopes all things, endures all things. (1 Corinthians 13:1-7)

And now these three remain: faith, hope, and love; but the greatest of these is love. (1 Corinthians 13:13)

Do everything in love. (1 Corinthians 16:14)

Let's briefly examine ourselves. Do we Love our spouse, children, friends, strangers, managers, or enemies? Hope and faith are wonderful and necessary, but they mean nothing without Love. If we can't or don't intentionally love one another, everything is futile. Remember the parable of the Good Samaritan, where Jesus was teaching on how to inherit eternal life (see Luke 10:30-37)? Who is your neighbor? Our neighbors are everyone alive, on or off this earth (I had to include the Astronauts). Since we see what Love is via the above scripture, let's see what Jesus instructs followers to do:

"You have heard that it was said, 'Love your neighbor' and 'Hate your enemy.' But I tell you, love your enemies and pray for those who persecute you, that you may be sons of your Father in heaven. He causes His sun to rise on the evil and the good and sends rain on the righteous and the unrighteous. If you love those

who love you, what reward will you get? Do not even tax collectors do the same? And if you greet only your brothers, what are you doing more than others? Do not even Gentiles do the same? Be perfect, therefore, as your heavenly Father is perfect." (Matthew 5:43-48)

But to those of you who will listen, I say: Love your enemies, do good to those who hate you, bless those who curse you, pray for those who mistreat you... If you love those who love you, what credit is that to you? Even sinners love those who love them... But love your enemies, do good to them, and lend to them, expecting nothing in return. Then your reward will be great, and you will be sons of the Most High; for He is kind to the ungrateful and wicked. Be merciful, just as your Father is merciful. (Luke 6:27,32,35-36)

And Paul in the Epistle to the Romans:

Be indebted to no one, except to one another in love. For he who loves his neighbor has fulfilled the law. The commandments "Do not commit adultery," "Do not murder," "Do not steal," "Do not covet," and any other commandments, are summed up in this one decree: "Love your neighbor as yourself." Love does no wrong to its neighbor. Therefore love is the fulfillment of the law. (Romans 13:8-10)

The bully from school, the evil neighbor that always tries taking your lawn furniture or garden gnomes, that coworker that constantly throws you under the bus, a boss that doesn't treat you well, the old friend that did you wrong, those that don't watch their language or content presented before children, etc., these people we shouldn't give the cold shoulder or silent treatment or forget the situations or any of the like. We are called to pray for all of them AND continue loving them. I have been learning more and more (even though my flesh and soul don't want me to) to love people regardless of their faults, quirks, temper, unawareness, reactions, etc. It doesn't matter how we were offended, that other person is too a child of God and deserves our love.

It is unfortunate, yet true, that we, in the body of Christ, often condemn each other. This past year, there were many scandals regarding Christian Leaders and there will probably be more in years to come. Instead of talking about them (gossiping) and saying negative things (not in love), we should pray for them instead (and not in a negative light). We should pray that God's perfect will for them be done. Help them, Lord! Help them understand the error of their ways, repent, come back to you, and sit at your feet! Why am I mentioning this? Well, I was one of these people until about a year ago. I might not agree with the building of multi-million-dollar parsonages or what people have done with whomever, but I cannot stand in judgment. I have to remember that I too, have made bad choices in life and have had my fair share of nay-sayers. As the Apostle Paul wrote to the Ephesians, we all have our part in the body, and because of this, we should love everyone no matter what.

Then we will no longer be infants, tossed about by the waves and carried around by every wind of teaching and by the clever cunning of men in their deceitful scheming. Instead, speaking the truth in love, we will in all things grow up into Christ Himself, who is the head. From Him the whole body, fitted and held together by every supporting ligament, grows and builds itself up in love through the work of each individual part. (Ephesians 4:14-16)

With all this in mind, we should look at what Jesus has to say regarding the body:

Your eye is the lamp of your body. When your eyes are good, your whole body also is full of light. But when they are bad, your body is full of darkness. Be careful, then, that the light within you is not darkness. So if your whole body is full of light, with no part of it in darkness, you will be radiant, as though a lamp were shining on you. (Luke 11:34-36)

The above words of Jesus don't mention Love, but there is a point in mentioning this scripture. If we don't have Love dwelling inside of us, then there is darkness dwelling in part of it. Therefore, if we don't walk in Love and see everything from the standpoint of Love, we are walking in darkness. One more revelation I have to mention is concerning the entire body of Christ. What I just mentioned also applies. It is so important that everyone, including all leaders and members of the five-fold ministry, strive to live what Jesus taught every day. Look at what happened to the couple (Ananias and Sapphira) in Acts Chapter 5, who sold their property but kept back some of the money from the church. They both died for lying to Apostle Peter, the Holy Spirit, and the entire 1st Century Church (see Acts 5:1-11). God doesn't play nice with liars; see what will happen at The Great White Throne Room Judgement:

But to the cowardly and unbelieving and abominable and murderers and sexually immoral and sorcerers and idolaters and all liars, their place will be in the lake that burns with fire and sulfur. This is the second death. (Revelation 21:8)

This scripture scared me straight in my walk with Christ. When you think of it, without all the layers of lies and hiding this and that, one can live freely in Christ. You will have nothing to worry about while living a pure life free of hate, lies, and sin, because there will be no darkness living inside of you. God designed the covenants with Adam, Moses, and Jesus to be free from sin and live this way, but our fallen nature has always gotten in the way. Luckily, after the fall of man, Jesus came and established the New Covenant. Now, we have the Holy Spirit as our helper, counselor, teacher, and guide. If it is hard for you to love someone else, ask God and the Holy Spirit for help.

Does Space/Distance Matter?

In the physical realm, we are bound by laws that govern how we move about and how fast. Look at when planning a family trip, what vehicle to take, how far to go, how fast to drive, where to stop, etc. In the physical, we are bound by space and time. When items come to the spiritual, time and space requirements are pretty different. The items mentioned after this sentence are based on my experiences and observations.

If I haven't mentioned this yet, I am part of the School of the Holy Spirit Church led by Thierry

Nakoa. One thing we do in the school is to have prayer rooms four times a day, Monday through Friday, on the Clubhouse audio app. In the prayer rooms, we offer prophecy to people who would like to hear a word from the Lord. One day, a person from each of these different countries and continents, the UK, Africa, and New Zealand, came up to receive a prophetic word in the prayer room I was in. I was still a student (and I am located in the USA). I did as always and leaned on and trusted the Holy Spirit for a word for each of them. To my surprise, everything we said to each one was completely on point. There are two things I learned from that experience. One is you don't have to lay hands on a person to speak a word to them. Number two, space doesn't matter in the spirit realm.

I have seen deliverances being performed and played back via YouTube before. I always thought one had to be in person for things to be effective. Thus, I was using logic and human brain power, which won't make sense with things of the spirit. Well, I have been through deliverances through electronic means (administering to others or others ministering to me) with outstanding success. This is example two: you don't have to have your hands laid on a person or be physically in the same room to cast out evil spirits. In conclusion, space doesn't matter in the spirit realm.

I have prayed for multiple friends and have picked up on something in the spirit. When I share with them what was seen or heard, they can relate directly to what was seen. Does this happen 100% of the time? Sadly, no, but I expect that to happen more often as I grow closer to the Lord. This is example three. You don't have to be physically in the same room to pray and get answers for someone. Again concluding, space doesn't matter in the spirit realm.

Jesus healed people from a distance (with no physical touch). See the stories about:

- The Centurion's Servant (Matthew 8:5-13 and Luke 7:1-10)
- Syro-Phoenician Woman's Daughter (Matthew 15:21-28 and Mark 7:24-30)
- The Capernaum Official's Son (John 4:46-54)

Another example is regarding Ananias being told by the Lord to go and baptize Paul in

Damascus (see Acts 9:10-16). In Acts Chapter 10, a Roman Centurion named Cornelius was visited by an angel and Peter was given a vision from the Lord in the same timeframe. If one thinks this is a coincidence, then how did Peter know Cornelius had sent for him and he was to go with the men? Well, the Lord told him not to consider things unholy, and he knew what it all meant when Cornelius' men showed up at his home (See Acts 10:1-23). Another story would be when the Holy Spirit fell on those sitting in the Upper Room on Pentecost (see Acts 2:1-4). I'm pretty sure they were all just praying. Then "BOOM!", the Holy Spirit fell on them and they started speaking in tongues. What does this all mean? In the words of Jesus:

> *"The wind blows where it wishes. You hear its sound, but you do not know where it comes from or where it is going. So it is with everyone born of the Spirit." (John 3:8)*

Before completely shutting out the idea of needing to be somewhere at the right time. Sometimes while we are at conferences or church services, we can receive impartations or activations. The same service or conference can be on YouTube, but when watched, the same thing won't happen as when in person. For example, I was at a couple of different conferences with some well-known speakers. At both conferences, they prayed over or toward a group of individuals (including myself), and I could feel a wave or a surge through my body, by the spirit. If a certain church has leaders that move in the gifts, they can impart something to you if led by the Lord. I have seen and heard this happen well more than once in different churches that do and don't move in the gifts of the Holy Spirit (sometimes purely by faith). Even reading books can give someone an impartation. Therefore, certain occult or adult content materials are dangerous to those unaware (especially children). They can get imparted something they aren't aware of by the spirit.

If one says, "Where is the word 'Impartation' in the Bible?" Well, it isn't there at all (unless a new translation I'm not aware of uses it). Bishop Bill Hamon of Christian International coined the word "Impartation" early in his ministry. It is called the laying on of hands in the New Testament. Jesus did this in Matthew 19:15, Mark 6:5, Mark 8:23, Mark 10:16, Luke 4:40, and Luke 13:13, just to name a few. This also happened later in the New

Testament in Acts 6:6, Acts 8:17, Acts 9:17, Acts 13:3, Acts 19:6, Acts 28:8, 1 Timothy 4:14, 2 Timothy 1:6, and Hebrews 6:2 to name a few more instances.

In conclusion, as mentioned above, the spiritual realm isn't bound by space. We, since we are physical beings, are bound by space and time. All things of the spirit are not bound by such things. Look at what the Apostle Peter says:

> *Beloved, do not let this one thing escape your notice: With the Lord, a day is like a thousand years, and a thousand years are like a day. (2 Peter 3:8)*

To God, a day is like a thousand years and a thousand years is like a day. I'm pretty sure science hasn't figured this one out. This number is probably larger, exponentially larger. Regardless of any scientific proof or not, just remember, the spirit realm and what it is composed of is outside of our physical space and time restraints.

Concluding Thoughts

God has put everything in perfect order. He has established laws and rules that we might not be 100% aware of yet. Through reading the Bible, studying the views of others, and personal observation, we can all better understand them. One thing to remember is that through all the laws and structure God has put in place, the enemy copies everything. That is why the mention of the Prince of Persia. He was the enemy's agent over a region used to try to stop God's angels from making it to Daniel.

Science is very important to humanity. It is used to figure out how the world works. We still haven't discovered everything about our planet; let alone the other planets we have been exploring via satellites, robots, drones, rovers, etc. There is always more with God. That is why we haven't discovered everything there is to know yet. The more we believe we have figured out, the more we find we didn't know beforehand.

Practical Application:

God has established laws and rules in the spirit and physical realm. As mentioned in Proverbs 25:2, God conceals and kings search out a matter. It is up to us to search out the items God has concealed. God grants those who want to do His will the ability to discover and understand certain mysteries.

- All modern sciences are studying what God has created and put into order.

- Faith and Hope fuels everything in the kingdom of God. Love is the driving force and is what connects us to God.

- To walk as a Christian, we need to walk in love always. If not, everything is futile.

- In the spirit realm, distance doesn't matter. Praying, prophesying, and deliverances don't have to take place in the same physical space.

- Being present in certain instances can be required if determined by the Lord. Sometimes, being in the right place at the right time holds true during impartations.

CHAPTER 4

———◆◇◆———

God's Kingdom Established

In the beginning, God created everything (the universe and everything in it). When God created man in their (Father, Son, Holy Spirit) image, what did God give man dominion over?

> *God blessed them and said to them, "Be fruitful and multiply, and fill the earth and subdue it; rule over the fish of the sea and the birds of the air and every creature that crawls upon the earth." Then God said, "Behold, I have given you every seed-bearing plant on the face of all the earth, and every tree whose fruit contains seed. They will be yours for food. (Genesis 1:28-29)*

Will you look at that? God loves his creation (man) so much, that He gave them dominion over everything. There is some revelation in the above verses. Look at what man has dominion over:

- Fish of the Sea
- Birds of the Sky
- Every living thing that moves on the Earth
- All plants yielding seed on the surface of the Earth
- All trees with fruit-yielding seed

Everything on the earth, in the sea, and the sky (within the first Heaven) is what man has been given dominion. All this includes the physical means of dominion. We were made to reign and rule over all creatures that roam or inhabit the earth. What about spiritual dominion within the first Heaven? Of course! If something is roaming around in our designated territory (the first heaven and earth), we have the authority to have it removed. God gave this authority to us when He created humanity. If something tries to make its way inside of us, we can reject it. If it is beyond something we can handle, then we call on God to take care of those issues for us. We shouldn't go seek things that have more strength or rank than we have; that is asking for trouble.

One big point I also want to make is to notice every plant yielding seed. What about every tree with fruit-yielding seed? What about those seedless fruits sold in stores? If God created them with seeds, why are there seedless varieties nowadays? Please excuse the tangent, but man did it and shouldn't have. Man has been playing with plant genetics for years (have you ever heard of GMO foods?). GMO differs from cross-pollination or grafting of trees. It is wrong, and man is playing God in a sense, and it should stop. Further talking about cloning humans and animals falls into alignment with this same principle. A big difference exists between having dominion and playing God, the creator. We should always stay in our lane and know when to act and when not to. Otherwise, we tread a thin line of disobedience. Let's dive into some examples of major events and order that were put in place by God because of the creation of humanity.

Garden of Eden

We mentioned in the earlier section, 'Created in the Image of God,' how Adam and the woman (Eve) weren't named until they were banished from the Garden of Eden. They were created on the sixth day of creation as mentioned in Genesis 1:26-31. Humanity was made to have dominion over the entire earth. This dominion was the first kingdom established by God on earth. Adam was spiritually and physically alive and working at 100% capacity of his entire being. One might ask, "How can one man name every creature, plant, fish, etc.?" Well, when we are all gifted with a supercomputer for a brain, if fully realized (we all have this natural capacity), anything is possible. Adam was operating 100% in the physical and spiritual. One could liken him to a superhero, but ideally, this is how humanity was initially designed to operate. Like our creator (when anything is possible) we are formed in His image and likeness. With Adam, there were no limits. Since Adam was the first and only man created and placed in the garden, he was king of that garden and technically the entire world (he did name every animal).

In the Garden of Eden, Adam was a king, and God created a helpmate for him. Adam named her woman (God later named her Eve). God gave them simple instructions for what to do and not to do in the garden (basically, enjoy yourselves, but stay away from that one tree). Now, with Adam and Eve, the first king and queen, essentially the first human kingdom was established on earth (figuratively speaking, this is not explicitly mentioned in the Bible).

Can you imagine walking in the cool of the day with God? How outstanding would that be? But alas, they were kicked out for being disobedient. Now, Adam and Eve are still king and queen of the earth, but can no longer live in the garden. They taught their children what to do to worship God and how to live, and then many generations went forth. A long time had happened before the next big event that God had planned for the world.

Post Great Flood

Before we discuss the after-the-flood, let's discuss Noah. He was a preacher of righteousness. Noah was also a type of Christ because he, by faith and obedience, built the arc and led his family through the purification of the world (known as the "Great Flood"). The symbology of the Great Flood is that the entire earth was baptized by water. The world was made anew through this process, like when a believer is water baptized.

Noah is a descendant of the line of Seth (Adam and Eve's third son). I won't review all the genealogy from Genesis Chapter 5, but the entire line of Noah's ancestors were priests to God and preachers of righteousness. The Book of Jasher explains more of this while paralleling the first books of the Bible (please don't be judgmental over the mention of Apocryphal books, I'm not talking about pulling rabbits from a hat or anything here, the Book of Jasher fills in many gaps the Bible doesn't cover over a certain period). This is important because, in the pre-flood world, there was an incredible amount of wickedness going on. The lineage of men from Seth to Noah is crucial because they lived holy lives as priests and kings to the Lord. Enoch was one descendant, and he walked so closely with God that he was taken up to heaven and didn't experience physical death.

And after he had become the father of Methuselah, Enoch walked with God 300 years and had other sons and daughters. So Enoch lived a total of 365 years. Enoch walked with God, and then he was no more, because God had taken him away. (Genesis 5:22-24)

When looking at the world post-flood, Noah is technically king of the world, a new world. This new world was purified from the previous world that was riddled with wickedness, giants, Nephilim, and the like. Once again, God establishes order just as in the garden with Adam, but the same issue occurs. Man still has their fallen nature.

Abraham's Promise

Everyone might remember the song "Father Abraham had many sons, many sons had father Abraham, I am one of them, and so are you...." Abraham might not be considered a figurative king of the world, but he was a friend of God. Abraham had an incredible walk of faith with God. He left his homeland. He went blindly wherever the Lord led him. There was a war between many kings of various cities and, with Abraham's help, there was victory and Melchizedek administered God's blessing to Abraham:

After Abram returned from defeating Chedorlaomer and the kings allied with him, the

71

king of Sodom went out to meet him in the Valley of Shaveh (that is, the King's Valley). Then Melchizedek king of Salem brought out bread and wine—since he was priest of God Most High and he blessed Abram and said: "Blessed be Abram by God Most High, Creator of heaven and earth, and blessed be God Most High, who has delivered your enemies into your hand." Then Abram gave Melchizedek a tenth of everything. The king of Sodom said to Abram, "Give me the people, but take the goods for yourself." But Abram replied to the king of Sodom, "I have raised my hand to the LORD God Most High, Creator of heaven and earth, that I will not accept even a thread, or a strap of a sandal, or anything that belongs to you, lest you should say, 'I have made Abram rich.' I will accept nothing but what my men have eaten and the share for the men who went with me— Aner, Eshcol, and Mamre. They may take their portion." (Genesis 14:17-24)

Because of Abraham's obedience, he received God's favor. Notice what Melchizedek brought out: bread and wine. Does this sound familiar? Did God's promises and favor in Abraham's life stop there? Not at all! Abraham was getting old of age and desired a son. God met Abraham where he was and made another covenant with him.

Abram continued, "Behold, You have given me no offspring, so a servant in my household will be my heir." Then the word of the LORD came to

Abram, saying, "This one will not be your heir, but one who comes from your own body will be your heir." And the LORD took him outside and said, "Now look to the heavens and count the stars, if you are able." Then He told him, "So shall your offspring be." Abram believed the LORD, and it was credited to him as righteousness. The LORD also told him, "I am the LORD, who brought you out of Ur of the Chaldeans to give you this land to possess."
(Genesis 15:3-7)

God then instructed Abraham on what sacrifices were needed to establish the covenant, and God made another promise.

As the sun was setting, Abram fell into a deep sleep, and suddenly great terror and darkness overwhelmed him. Then the LORD said to Abram, "Know for certain that your descendants will be strangers in a land that is not their own, and they will be enslaved and mistreated four hundred years. But I will judge the nation they serve as slaves, and afterward they will depart with many possessions. You, however, will go to your fathers in peace and be buried at a ripe old age. In the fourth generation your descendants will return here, for the iniquity of the Amorites is not yet complete." (Genesis 15:12-16)

For those who know their Bibles, this is a prophecy of the Hebrew bondage in Egypt and the book of Exodus. Now, Abraham had two sons,

Ishmael by Hagar and Isaac by Sarah. It is essential to understand the significance of Ishmael and Isaac. Hagar was Sarah's servant, which made her a slave or a bondwoman. Ishmael was born because of man trying to fulfill a promise from God. We might have good intentions, but sometimes our actions aren't what God had intended. God's ways are higher than our ways. I suppose if we do things His way, there will be no issues. Either way, God promised to bless both Ishmael and Isaac by making many nations from their offspring. Over time, Sarah grew tired of Hagar and didn't approve of them all staying together. So, Abraham sent Hagar and Ishmael away after some years. Then God commanded Abraham to sacrifice Isaac, now his only son. When Abraham went to do so, guess what happened?

> *Then Abraham reached out his hand and took the knife to slaughter his son. Just then the angel of the LORD called out to him from heaven, "Abraham, Abraham!" "Here I am," he replied. "Do not lay a hand on the boy or do anything to him," said the angel, "for now I know that you fear God, since you have not withheld your only son from me." (Genesis 22:10-12)*

Since Abraham feared the Lord, the promise was further set in stone (figuratively speaking).

> And the angel of the LORD called to Abraham from heaven a second time, saying, "By Myself I have sworn, declares the LORD, that because you have done this and have not withheld your only son, I will surely bless you, and I will multiply your descendants like the stars in the sky and the sand on the seashore. Your descendants will possess the gates of their enemies. And through your offspring all nations of the earth will be blessed, because you have obeyed My voice." (Genesis 22:15-18)

Notice that God made a promise/vow by Himself to Abraham. Why or how can God do this? There is nothing above Him. He is the creator of the universe and everything. He can't make a promise/vow to anything greater, excellent, or more significant than Him because no such thing exists. This means that if God breaks His vow, He is then amounted to nothing and shamed, which cannot happen.

> God is not a man, that He should lie, or a son of man, that He should change His mind. Does He speak and not act? Does He promise and not fulfill? (Numbers 23:19)

One must wonder why these promises are being listed? God hand-picked one man with no home.

75

One man who had total faith and trust in Him. One man, through his offspring, would create a people that would love and serve God. Now, to link back to the earlier section, "On Earth as in Heaven," Abraham has created a Covenant with God. By Abraham's faith in God, which was credited to him as righteousness, through all the promises God gave Abraham.

Abraham's faith made him a friend of God. Abraham saw what was coming, but did not live to see it. It was through his grandson Jacob (whose name became 'Israel') and Jacob's sons that all the tribes of Israel were established. After they became slaves in a strange land, even though they kept their traditions, they went backward (into living in/with sin) instead of forward (righteousness). When have you dealt with or lived with some sin? It could be little, but you were tolerant of it. Though minor or little, if it is sin, then how do you think God feels about it? Sin is still sin. We should avoid it at all costs.

Concluding Thoughts

Through all the ups and downs, God is still with and for His creation. Adam and Eve severely messed up in the garden by not keeping their guard up. The result was that the world turned into being full of wickedness and lawlessness. Many bad things were happening in the world. That is why God had to bring the Great Flood and how we get the story of Noah's Ark. Abraham was considered a friend of God. Through Abraham's faith, his obedience to God was great. Abraham fully believed in the promises of God. Through the covenant between God and Abraham, we now live by faith and not works.

Practical Application:

Multiple examples from the Old Testament apply to us today. By examining the relationships between individuals in the Bible, one can determine how God will act or react.

- Like Adam, if one doesn't steward their responsibilities well and walks in disobedience, the direct result is separation from God.

- Noah led people into a new world through the ark that took him over 100 years to build. The problem was that man's fallen nature still got in the way and perverted the earth again.

  o You can lead people in the correct way. It is up to them to stay the course.

- Men ought to not try to make promises of God come true on their timing. If so, the promise will be like Ishmael and birthed in bondage.

  o Rather, we should wait for God's word and will to be done, then the promise will be like Isaac, a blessing.

- Faith and a relationship with God will draw you close to Him, like Abraham, who communed with God often. Nurture that relationship of faith with God and watch what He will do.

CHAPTER 5

---◄○►---

The Ten Commandments

Anyone that has read the Bible knows about Moses. If anyone wants to know who Moses is, please read Exodus Chapters 2-3 (and further, if desired). God used Moses to bring His people out of Egypt to the promised land (what was promised to Abraham and his descendants). One catch was the people had to wander through the wilderness before reaching the promised land. During this wilderness experience, God set up the Ten Commandments and the rest of the "Law" or "Law of Moses." The Law comprised 613 laws and ordinances the people had to live by. For this section's sake; we will only discuss the Ten Commandments. I'm sure everyone has heard of the commandments before. If not, then buckle your seatbelts. We are about to break down the Ten Commandments and explain what they all mean. Before we start, I have to mention that the original intention of the commandments was to reveal to the Hebrew people what sin actually was. Remember, the people still lived in a fallen world full of sin and deceit. Jesus hadn't come to bring salvation to the world, so everyone was still slaves to sin from the fall of man.

What then shall we say? Is the law sin? Certainly not! Indeed, I would not have been mindful of sin if not for the law. For I would not have been aware of coveting if the law had not said, "Do not covet." (Romans 7:7)

Notice the verse above from Romans; the people didn't know what sin was until they had the Law established. I'm pointing this out because this section of Romans explains how sin took advantage of the people. How did this happen? Have you ever heard the saying "Curiosity killed the cat?" In the Old Testament, the people were like cats, curious about what the Laws meant and sometimes deliberately sought to break them. Some horrific examples in the Old Testament are why Sodom and Gomorrah were destroyed (see Genesis 18:16 through Genesis 19:5, there were not 10 righteous people there, otherwise the Lord would have spared the city (Genesis 18:32)), what the Benjamites did to the Levite's concubine in Gibeah (see Judges Chapters 19-20, this caused a Civil War within Israel (Judges 20:18-48) and a division from the Tribe of Benjamin (Judges 21:1-4)), the turning away from God to other gods like Ba'al and the like (this happened too many times to list specific scripture references), etc. In summary, if there was a king or not, the people naturally still wanted to sin. If one broke the law, it was punishable by death. Back then, the people of the area/region, town, or city would publicly stone the person (man, woman, or child) to death. Below is how the people's transgressions would be handled per the instructions given by Moses:

A lone witness is not sufficient to establish any wrongdoing or sin against a man, regardless of what offense he may have committed. A matter must be established by the testimony of two or three witnesses. If a false witness testifies against someone, accusing him of a crime, both parties to the dispute must stand in the presence of the

> *LORD, before the priests and judges who are in office at that time. The judges shall investigate thoroughly, and if the witness is proven to be a liar who has falsely accused his brother, you must do to him as he intended to do to his brother. So you must purge the evil from among you. Then the rest of the people will hear and be afraid, and they will never again do anything so evil among you. You must show no pity: life for life, eye for eye, tooth for tooth, hand for hand, and foot for foot. (Deuteronomy 19:15-21)*

Part of that last verse, "An eye for an eye, a tooth for a tooth," is such a dangerous expression. Some use that as a justification of revenge or even being a vigilante. The whole point was to make a public spectacle of the issue so people knew what not to do. In the book of Deuteronomy, there are more instances and examples of righteous living as defined by Moses (which wrote the words given to him by God). Since we now live in the New Covenant, we shouldn't throw everything aside as useless. The Old Covenant is the basis of the New Covenant and still applies today. We will get to that in the next section, called "Sermon on the Mount."

Now that we have some history out of the way, let's review the Ten Commandments.

First Commandment

You shall have no other gods before Me. (Exodus 20:3)

Many civilizations of that time worshipped many gods. They also worshipped gods that required animal, human, child, or baby sacrifices (these deities are still in operation today). Doing these types of sacrifices gave them power. Our God, Yahweh, Jehovah, the I Am That I Am (YHWH) loves His people and didn't require human sacrifice in the Old Testament. He has always loved His chosen people. He might have been angry with them multiple times, but He still loved them.

Second Commandment

You shall not make for yourself an idol in the form of anything in the heavens above, on the earth below, or in the waters beneath. You shall not bow down to them or worship them; for I, the LORD your God, am a jealous God, visiting the iniquity of the fathers on their children to the third and fourth generations of those who hate Me, but showing loving devotion to a thousand generations of those who love Me and keep My commandments. (Exodus 20:4-6)

Idols can be anything that takes precedence over God. Nowadays, idols can be anything from sports teams, a spouse, children, work, hobbies, movie stars, music artists, ourselves, social media, etc. Notice how scripture says to not make anything and submit to them. Submission means that they dictate what you do and they will lead your life.

I'm a car guy. I know and have met so many people that live, breathe, and sweat working on their show cars and taking them to shows. People will say "Oh, that is just Johnny. He is washing and waxing his car just like last week. He has a big car show on Sunday again. That is just what he does." Meanwhile, Johnny's wife and children don't spend enough time with him and his children grow to dislike cars. All of this is because Johnny has made his show car an idol. Speaking of car guys, some actors or popular figures have entire collections of antique or classic cars and big houses, sometimes these are their idols, sometimes not.

The litmus test is to ask yourself, what drives me every day? What are my daily thoughts focused on? When I have worries, what/who do I run to for comfort? If I am at my lowest of low, what/who can bring me out of it? If I have had enough and just want to get away from everything and everyone, what do I need to focus on to just get lost in and not have to worry about the rest of the world? If it is something other than God, some self-reflection needs to take place.

Before moving on, I want to mention that people such as a spouse, friend, children, pastor, brother/sister, manager, etc. are all good to have in your life. They can help you through tough times and even give you joy and happiness. The question is, does your life revolve around only them and serving solely them and nothing else? If so, they are an idol. I mention this because many people turn to drugs, alcohol, promiscuous or provocative behaviors, and other items or behaviors to fulfill themselves to remove themselves from the world. Look at Narcissists, everything will and should revolve around them or the world will crumble (this is their thought pattern). Narcissists do this and bring others down to a level of submission unless healthy boundaries are set. Where am I going with this? Some people try to make themselves an idol

(Narcissists), some turn to drugs, some turn to friends for comfort, some unfortunately turn to satanic/pagan practices because they get instant results without knowing/realizing the end consequences. It is an endless spiral of emptiness unless one turns to God and keeps their gaze fixed on Him. Many are a pure product of this, myself included. I used to drown myself in a bottle or mixed drinks and do things I knew I shouldn't have. I became a slave to it; it was my idol at that point in my life. Was I able to overcome under my own power? Yes, to a point and for a long time. That, my friends, is called coping and is not a permanent solution. The problem was that it was solely under my own power, and at times, I wanted to go back to it. But when God comes in like a flood, you get a taste of the Holy Spirit, there is no turning back. Our gaze and our everything should always be toward Him, nothing or no one else. Okay, making idols out of something or someone; that is bad, very bad, let's continue on.

Third Commandment

You shall not take the name of the LORD your God in vain, for the LORD will not leave anyone unpunished who takes His name in vain. (Exodus 20:7)

Oh, but yet another sin I used to have rule my life. I had the mouth of a sailor. It is so amazing to me at how many people use the Lord's name in vain (especially during self-reflection of myself). G## ### ## (with some other phraseology and word usage usually before, during, or after it) is a common phrase I hear people say, sometimes multiple times a day or even the same sentence (and not by accident). Truthfully, I used to say this a lot. In some places I used to live, it was and still is a common expression. Now when I hear it said, it is like scratching a chalkboard to my ears. Society has reduced themselves down to a point of saying this phrase as part of their regular daily vocabulary and language usage. And people are totally okay with it. The enemy has so crept in and perverted so much; we have to abstain from saying foul speech. What do the words of King Soloman say:

He who guards his mouth protects his life, but the one who opens his lips invites his own ruin. (Proverbs 13:3)

A soothing tongue is a tree of life, but a perverse tongue crushes the spirit. (Proverbs 15:4)

Better a poor man who walks with integrity than a fool whose lips are perverse. (Proverbs 19:1)

There are many other verses mentioned in the Bible to support this commandment. One more scripture that is worth mentioning is:

But I tell you that men will give an account on the day of judgment for every careless word they have spoken. For by your words you will be acquitted, and by your words you will be condemned." (Matthew 12:36-37)

Words coming straight from Jesus' mouth. This warning needs to be taken with the utmost care. It is not enough to abstain from blaspheming the name of God, but all other forms of filthy language aren't acceptable. Read again the words that Jesus spoke in the Gospel according to Matthew and meditate/think on it for a while. Every idle word is anything from perversion, hate, dissention, gossip, anything that is not of God. If this is part of your daily or occasional speech with certain friend groups, search your heart to see where it truly is. Are you living to glorify God? Are you wanting to be accepted by groups of friends? Can speaking of God wait until church service or until only at home? It is your choice and between you and God, what you do and don't accept. God hears, sees, and knows all (even your thoughts). Yielding what you say is better than speaking idle words until any heart issues are dealt with.

Fourth Commandment

Remember the Sabbath day by keeping it holy. Six days you shall labor and do all your work, but the seventh day is a Sabbath to the LORD your God, on which you must not do any work—neither you, nor your son or daughter, nor your manservant or maidservant or livestock, nor the foreigner within your gates. For in six days the LORD made the heavens and the earth and the sea and all that is in them, but on the seventh day He rested. Therefore the LORD blessed the Sabbath day and set it apart as holy. (Exodus 20:8-11)

The sabbath day, this can be up for debate by most people. The sabbath day is not merely speaking of the day one would attend a church. In Jewish culture, and also according to Merriam-Webster, Saturday is the seventh day of the week.[10] Traditionally in the Jewish culture, the sabbath day would be Saturday and then Sunday would be the day to worship God at the temple. I want to keep emphasizing, this was traditional to the Jewish culture at the time the Old and New

---

[10] "Definition of SATURDAY."

Testaments were written. One might ask, then why do churches meet at different times of the week, even on Saturdays? Why do New Covenant believers not follow this commandment? I will dwell here to state that whether someone is a Christian (New Covenant) or if one still believes in the Old Covenant laws and rules, taking a day off from work to spend with God is not frowned upon. We should clear out our schedules for God, to allow Him to move in our lives and set aside our agendas. In the New Covenant (modern day Christians), God wants 100% of our everything. If we constantly have Him in or on the mind, we will live for Him and not ourselves. Again, it is all about heart posture. We in the western world live very busy lives, with full calendars seven days a week. The key questions to ask are "Is God part of your daily calendar/routine?" and "Are you living for the glory of God or to glorify yourself and those around you?" Is whatever turned toward Him to fulfill His plans and purposes? Are you living a life pleasing to God? We can find ourselves so wrapped up in many activities, we need to always ensure we are focused on God in and through all things.

Fifth Commandment

Honor your father and mother, so that your days may be long in the land that the LORD your God is giving you. (Exodus 20:12)

Looking back in the times of the Old Testament, especially around the timeframe of Exodus, children probably didn't have a lot of respect for their parents or older people. Growing up in Egypt, there were a lot of bad things going on. The Egyptians were way different from the Hebrew people. They lived immorally and practiced occult things daily. Nowadays, some cultures ingrain a total respect for elders, even if they are a day older than you. I was not raised to strictly respect elders; it was more natural to me. I had my fair share of correction from saying or doing something wrong as a child (bars of soap and belts weren't my friends). In my case, it allowed me to grow up with a respect to older people, such as grandparents or older neighbors. As for parents, I had experienced a rebellious streak when younger. Now, looking back as a parent myself, I was pretty foolish (I thought I knew what was good for me).

Looking back at the time of Moses, this must have been a big deal to God. If a child disrespected their mother or father, they would be stoned to death by the entire camp, village, city, etc. I would be safe to say this probably also accounted for the elderly. What if this was the mentality nowadays, especially in the American Public School system? I remember when kids could be paddled for being bad or out of line. That always made you think twice before talking back to a teacher. Now, the children are almost running the show and making the rules. It is truly a shame. I grew up in a small town with a lot of elderly widows and couples. We always treated them with respect and you received the same in return.

Sixth Commandment

You shall not murder. (Exodus 20:13)

The one commandment that seems like a no-brainer, do not murder anyone. If you remember how Moses originally left Egypt, he killed an Egyptian taskmaster that was beating a Hebrew (see Exodus 2:11-12). It is not mentioned explicitly, but there were a lot of dangers when traveling back then. Robbers would wait and kill you for your goods or money. That is why the patriarchs (Abraham, Isaac, and Jacob) and their applicable kinfolk had trained men for protection. The issue of the day was that righteous living wasn't the normal way of life. Look at Adam and Eve's first two sons, Cain and Abel. Cain killed Abel because Abel's sacrifice was pleasing to God and his wasn't. Think about it, the two people that communed personally and walked with God in the Garden of Eden with no restraints (Adam and Eve). Their firstborn son killed the other one. How terrible was that day? God even warned Cain by speaking to him about his feelings (see Genesis 4:3-8). The role of a parent is very important to create that foundation of righteousness for the children of this earth to follow. Overall, God was setting the stage to let His people know that in order to live righteous and holy and pleasing to Him, murder was and is out of the question.

Seventh Commandment

You shall not commit adultery. (Exodus 20:14)

For those that might not know what adultery is, it is a married person being intimate with someone other than their spouse. There are examples of this in the Bible that happened before the ten commandments were given to the Israelites at Mount Sinai. One reason why there was the great flood was because of all the unlawfulness and wickedness going on in the earth. The Bible doesn't explicitly state that there was adultery going on, but I'd be safe to assume there was. Sodom and Gomorrah were destroyed because they were exceedingly wicked and sinned heavily. In Genesis Chapter 19, it explains that the men of Sodom wanted to have relations with the visitors (angels of God) that were in Lot's house. I'm sure the men of Sodom were married and had children. They had large male only orgies, and newcomers were probably ravished to death, based on:

> *Before they had gone to bed, all the men of the city of Sodom, both young and old, surrounded the house. They called out to Lot, saying, "Where are the men who came to you tonight? Send them out to us so we can have relations with them!" (Genesis 19:4-5)*

Later on, the people of Sodom and Gomorrah met their doom. Moving forward to Egypt while Joseph was a slave in Potiphar's house, Potiphar's wife tried multiple times to have Joseph lie with her per Genesis 39:10. Since Joseph was righteous, even though a slave, he constantly resisted and ignored her. One day she trapped him and took his garment, made up a lie, and got Joesph thrown into prison (even though he ran away from the situation and was innocent). Joseph was in the right and God later redeemed him.

Going back to God's original design of marriage between man and woman, this is very sacred in His eyes. A lot of big named pastors, leaders, and the like are being exposed for scandals involving adultery. Some cultures even allow this. Certain religions even allow multiple wives. Per the Bible in the Old Covenant under the law, they had laws regarding what could and couldn't be done. The main point of this commandment is a man and a woman are to be married per God's original design. That same man and woman are supposed to be faithful to each other, end of discussion in God's eyes.

Eighth Commandment

You shall not steal. (Exodus 20:15)

One other way of living righteously is not being a thief. Examples of stealing would be in Genesis with Jacob. It was thought Jacob stole his brother Esau's birthright. Esau actually gave up his inheritance to Jacob for a bowl of soup (see Genesis 25:29-34). Per Jacob's mother Rebekah, she helped dress him up and Jacob stole Esau's blessing (See Genesis Chapter 27). When Jacob returned home after fleeing for his life, he ended up with two wives that were sisters, Leah and Rachel, instead of the original one he desired. Although allowed at that time, obtaining two wives was from deceit from his Uncle Laban (Rebekah's brother) to keep Jacob there for longer so Laban could prosper (see Genesis Chapters 29-30). Later, Rachel stole Laban's household idols when Jacob, his wives, his children, his servants, and his flocks of animals all fled to go back to Canaan (see Genesis 31:19 and 34-35). Later, Jacob had his favorite son, Joseph, taken away because his brothers hated him and sold him into slavery (see Genesis 37:18-28). I mention all of this because of Rebekah's family line. This was something consistent with them. Jacob had many hardships in life because of thievery on his part and from others, including his own family (and children). Remember earlier that God will visit the iniquity of the sons up to the fourth generation (see Exodus 34:6-7), that means habits of sin are passed down to future generations unless the parents/children take a stand to remove the sin from their family line (become chain breakers). In order to live righteously, we shall not steal. Some cultures, and even movies, show how people caught stealing would get their hand or arm cut off. In the USA, someone caught stealing can go to jail. Whether in the Bible or a nation's laws, not stealing is an important rule to live by.

Nineth Commandment

You shall not bear false witness against your neighbor. (Exodus 20:16)

Bearing false witness. What does this mean? Bearing a false witness is saying something untrue about someone. If one has ever watched any movies involving courtrooms in America, whomever goes up to the witness stand has to put their hand on a Bible and pledge that they will say nothing but the truth (paraphrasing). If someone lies on the witness stand, that is called perjury in the USA. Perjury is a crime punishable by law. I listed a scripture above from Deuteronomy Chapter 19, stating that a single witness could not be used. Reason is because one could lie and condemn someone's life, so at least two to three people have to be used to ensure justice was administered fairly to the people.

Bearing false witness can also be starting a false rumor about someone. Have you ever played that game as a child in school where the teacher would share something with the first child? The first child would then share with the next, and the next, and so on until coming back to the teacher. One hundred percent of the time, the teacher would not get the same message repeated back to them. Think about what will happen if someone starts a rumor about someone they don't like? It could escalate to something pretty outlandish, correct? This very thing has happened to many people. Some are still in prison over it or have had to live with shame for a very long time until the truth is revealed. This is not a cultural or territorial thing; it is a human issue directly resulting from our fallen nature. Review the three verses from Proverbs above regarding Commandment #3 of not using the Lord's name in vain (see Proverbs 13:3 and 15:4 and 19:1). It is a good thing to control our tongues and what comes out of our mouths. Speaking the truth and nothing less is always pleasing in the eyes of God. It is also good for society and the entirety of humanity if all would follow this principle.

Tenth Commandment

You shall not covet your neighbor's house. You shall not covet your neighbor's wife, or his manservant or maidservant, or his ox or donkey, or anything that belongs to your neighbor. (Exodus 20:17)

I know I mentioned the word 'covet' before and it is also mentioned throughout the Bible. Merriam-Webster defines 'covet' as:

to wish for earnestly

to desire (what belongs to another) inordinately or culpably[11]

What would it cause in someone that wishes earnestly for something that someone else has? I would be safe to say that coveting would lead to jealousy and envy. I'm sure we all have been there before, seeing something someone else has and we say "I wish I had...." It could be a new vehicle, a home they just bought or built, a new motorcycle, computer, gaming console, pet, girl/boyfriend,

---

[11] "Definition of COVET."

family members, handbag, clothes, etc. The list could go on almost forever. In America, it is common for many couples to drive through certain neighborhoods and look at the large houses and daydream about owning them and making it a lifestyle to live like those more fortunate and they always struggle (people refer to this as "keeping up with the Jones'"). When I was younger, I wish I had a friend's parents as relatives. Truly, there were times I wished some friend's parents were my own. We all might brush some things like this off as we were young and know better now. Though it is true, we should all look a little deeper to check ourselves and see "How appreciative are we of what we have been given?" Have you ever had something you appreciated so much that someone asked "Why do you take care of that so much?" or "Why do you wash and wax your car (or truck) every week?" If you do it all out of appreciation for what you have, then you are doing a good thing. If you make it your constant focus and it becomes an idol, that is when a realignment needs to happen.

Moving back to envy and jealousy, these can hinder you during your walk. If they hadn't, then

CHAPTER 5: The Ten Commandments

God wouldn't have prescribed his people to follow this as one of the ten commandments.

Concluding Thoughts

The Hebrew People were given the Ten Commandments directly from God. These were to establish a guideline, so the people knew how to live righteously and holy. The problem was the people still naturally had a fallen nature and fell into sin constantly, normally by choice. The Ten Commandments and the law was made in case someone accidentally broke it. The problem became people just did it and then gave sacrifices later as an atonement for their sins. This didn't generate righteous and holy living, but an endless cycle of religion. Do you practice the same thing over and over religiously to feel accepted by God? That is religion. God wants us to be sons and daughters and walk with Him. When you walk, it isn't always the same terrain, is it? What I am saying is the walk will always be changing. If we continually get stuck in a cycle of doing the same things, we need to self-examine ourselves to ensure we aren't caught up in any religious cycle leading to nowhere.

Practical Application:

Many people might state that the Old Testament doesn't apply to New Testament believers. I don't fully believe in that statement. The Old Testament gives us plenty of examples of what to do and what not to do in life. Regarding many examples from the Old Testament, the following could apply to any believer:

- God created the Ten Commandments and established the Mosaic Law so the people would have a guideline to live righteous and holy lives.

- If a little bit of sin can enter in or is tolerated, it will grow like a well-watered weed.

- Sin can compare to how frogs are cooked. They won't jump into a boiling pot of water (just like we won't knowingly walk into sin or a dangerous situation). But if the frog is put in the water and it is heated slowly, they won't jump out and will become cooked, and ultimately, food.

  o We are the frogs, able to jump out at any time.

  o Sin is the water. If the water is boiling (sin is active and viewable), we will avoid it at all costs. If the water starts off as cold and warms up, that is us tolerating that sin until it overtakes us. Then, we become cooked frogs (not realizing what was happening, blind to the situations, and never jumping out to be saved).

CHAPTER 6

Sermon on the Mount

Many people believe that all modern-day Christians don't need to worry about what is written in the Old Testament. Please excuse the repetitions, but I have heard this a lot: "Since Christianity is based on Jesus' ministry, death, burial, and resurrection, none of the Old Testament should apply." This thought pattern is totally false. We must read and understand the content of both the Old and New Testaments to fully realize the intent of the Bible. I always say that the Old Testament is like a strategy guide for

New Testament believers. We must understand the history of the Hebrew people in the Old Testament, the many things that happened, and the results to relate to modern times and events currently in our lives. In the words of King Solomon, the wisest king of all time:

> *What has been will be again, and what has been done will be done again; there is nothing new under the sun. (Ecclesiastes 1:9)*
>
> *It is the glory of God to conceal a matter and the glory of kings to search it out. (Proverbs 25:2)*

If one stumbles upon something mentioned in the Bible, there is probably a story to back it up or explain it in further detail elsewhere. Also, whatever is happening in one's life right now, there is probably a story in the Bible that mirrors or can be related to it. If one genuinely wants to discover secrets to eternal life, search the scriptures to know how to live. God had neatly included them in the Bible for us to seek and find them.

The previous section relating to the Old Covenant and the Ten Commandments directly correlates with most of the fundamentals Jesus teaches about in the New Testament. Technically, the New Covenant didn't begin until the Book of Acts. The four gospels (Matthew, Mark, Luke, and John) all explain the story of Jesus from their perspective. We will start with the teachings of Jesus from Matthew's perspective.

First, why did we cover the Ten Commandments in the previous section? The Hebrew people (including Jesus) lived under the Law of Moses and the Ten Commandments. Understanding the Ten Commandments and how ineffective they were due to the people's mindset and the teachings of Jesus will start to make sense shortly. In the Old Covenant, the people would sin and give offerings to be forgiven. The whole point was to point them towards living a holy and righteous life. Why was this not obtainable?

Why then was the law given? It was added because of transgressions, until the arrival of the seed to whom the promise referred. It was administered through angels by a mediator. A mediator is unnecessary, however, for only one party; but God is one. Is the law, then, opposed to the promises of God? Certainly not! For if a law had been given that could impart life, then righteousness would certainly have come from the law. (Galatians 3:19-21)

107

Aha, the law was given until the arrival of the seed to whom the promise is referred. To what promise? The promise of Abraham (see Genesis 22:15-18) which includes that his descendants will possess the gates of their enemies and the entire earth will be blessed. Most of the Hebrews believed this was pointing to a great general and they would trample down their physical enemies. Jesus came because he had to make all the wrong things right. He had to correct the fall of man. Jesus came to teach the ways of God so all people would understand what the Law of Moses was supposed to of led to. Let us dive into the teachings of Jesus from his Sermon on the Mount

The Beatitudes

"Blessed are the poor in spirit, for theirs is the kingdom of heaven.

Blessed are those who mourn, for they will be comforted.

Blessed are the meek, for they will inherit the earth.

Blessed are those who hunger and thirst for righteousness, for they will be filled.

Blessed are the merciful, for they will be shown mercy.

Blessed are the pure in heart, for they will see God.

Blessed are the peacemakers, for they will be called sons of God.

Blessed are those who are persecuted because of righteousness, for theirs is the kingdom of heaven.

Blessed are you when people insult you, persecute you, and falsely say all kinds of evil against you because of Me. Rejoice and be glad, because great is your reward in heaven; for in the same way they persecuted the prophets before you." *(Matthew 5:3-12)*

Jesus starts out his famous sermon on the Mount by describing a Christian's lifestyle and character. As we break each of these down, self-reflect on where you stand with each one of these sections.

- 'Poor in Spirit' refers to a person who is not self-sufficient and must rely on the grace of God. This type of person lives in humility and knows their need for a savior. Someone with an "I can do it all by myself" attitude doesn't fit this category. It is very noteworthy that Jesus mentioned the very category dealing with the grace of God first. Requiring the grace of God in our lives is further solidified and explained in the New Testament Epistles.

- 'Those who mourn' don't refer to a consistently sad person. The mourning is in relation to when one sins. What will their reaction be? Will they say, "Oh well, I'm covered by grace and can do whatever I want" or will they truly be sorry of their actions? The ones that truly recognize the errors of their ways and turn from sin will be comforted. What kind of comfort will they receive? They will receive the forgiveness of God and the salvation through Jesus Christ.

- Those who are 'meek' don't refer to those that are weak and feeble. Meekness mentioned by Jesus is a person under full control of the Holy Spirit. Being under full control of the spirit doesn't make someone weak, it actually makes them strong. How does it make one strong? Paul mentions in 1 Corinthians that he has his body under full submission, meaning the building up of his spirit man to be a heavyweight, not an adolescent (see 1 Corinthians 9:24-27).

- 'Those who hunger and thirst for righteousness' are those that live for God's righteousness. This type of people does not seek their own righteousness nor are self-righteous. The Pharisees are a great example of self-righteous people. One must live continuously for God's righteousness to manifest in their lives to become fully satisfied.

- The 'merciful' is pretty self-explanatory. If a person forgives others, especially other brothers and sisters, our Father will forgive them. This theme is common in the New Testament and Jesus covers this in a few parables (see Matthew 18:21-35 and Luke 16:19-31).

- The 'pure in heart' is also self-explanatory. Those that are sincere and do not have ill motives and always want the best for others, they will see God!

- The 'peacemakers' are those that love unconditionally. Peacemakers must always keep their mind and emotions in check and fully submitted to the Holy Spirit.

- 'Those who are persecuted because of righteousness' is a martyr. Is Jesus calling Christians to be a martyr? Absolutely not, but if something happens in our walk and we have to deny the faith or be persecuted, beat, whipped, tortured, etc. we should be ready for the latter. Look at what happened to all the Twelve Apostles in Acts (including Paul), all but John was killed in one form or another. Peter was

111

crucified upside-down (as requested).[12]   The romans tried killing John the Apostle in a cauldron of boiling oil and he came out with fresh skin like a newborn baby.   That is why John was exiled to the island of Patmos.   The Romans couldn't kill him![13]

- When people are insulted, persecuted, and have false things said about them because of Jesus, they shall have a substantial reward in heaven. Again, this falls back on our last point.   In the early church, Christians were heavily persecuted. Currently, in parts of the world, the same thing would happen to Christians.   As mentioned above about martyrs, we should not actively go looking for trouble.   If trouble (insults, persecution, false accusations, etc.) comes your way, endure it with love and forgiveness for those doing/saying it. Remember, Jesus forgave everyone when he was nailed to the cross (see Luke 23:34).   We should do the same.

Jesus is setting a pretty high standard, especially for that day.   Look at what happened after his

---

[12] "How Did St. Peter Die?"

[13] "Saint John the Apostle | Biography, Facts, Feast Day, Writings, & Death | Britannica."

ministry. He was crucified! During the entire account of Jesus in all four gospels, he adhered to these standards. All Christians are to live by these standards through the help of the Holy Spirit. Jesus was preaching this not just for those around him on that very day; but for all those that would become Christians after the inception of the church in Acts Chapter 2.

Salt of the Earth

"You are the salt of the earth. But if the salt loses its savor, how can it be made salty again? It is no longer good for anything, except to be thrown out and trampled by men." (Matthew 5:13)

Jesus is referring to the people as salt. What does salt do?

- Salt enhances the flavor of foods.
- Salt preserves food (they didn't have refrigerators back then).
- Salt can be used as a cleaning agent.
- Salt can be used in various ways in the kitchen.
- Salt can kill certain plants.
- Salt can repel certain insects.
- Salt can maintain our health (electrolytes).

- Salt can remove stains from clothes and set colors.

The list of uses of salt can go on and on. How does this compare to human beings, especially Christians? Would it be safe to say that a Christian can help clean themselves by the washing of the Word of God? What about preserving themselves when times get rough? What about removal of stains, repelling things that aren't supposed to be in their lives, etc.? Jesus is calling us all to level-up. Jesus is calling us to live righteously and holy through the help of the Holy Spirit. He is calling us to walk like He walked on the earth. The whole point of the gospels and Jesus' ministry was to give us a perfect example of how to walk on the earth.

What happens if we lose our saltiness? What happens if we decide to stop living and walking as Christians? Jesus says it would make us worthless and fit to be trampled under men. How terrible would that be? Look at the church today. There has been much light shown to expose darkness and many issues being revealed. I believe this is what Jesus is alluding to. People get in a place or position and then complacency settles in. We need to always be in a place of accountability with other brothers and sisters in the community, always self-improving. These words of Jesus parallel what is written in Hebrews:

> *It is impossible for those who have once been enlightened, who have tasted the heavenly gift, who have shared in the Holy Spirit, who have tasted the goodness of the word of God and the powers of the coming age—and then have fallen away—to be restored to repentance, because they themselves are crucifying the Son of God all over again and subjecting Him to open shame. (Hebrews 6:4-6)*

Let us not subject Jesus to open shame. Instead, let us keep fighting the good fight and not give up our position!

Light of the World

> *"You are the light of the world. A city on a hill cannot be hidden. Neither do people light a lamp and put it under a basket. Instead, they set it on a stand, and it gives light to everyone in the house. In the same way, let your light shine before men, that they may see your good deeds and glorify your Father in heaven." (Matthew 5:14-16)*

Remember that in Genesis Chapter One, God spoke, and there was light. The light was good and separated itself from the darkness. The followers of Jesus, Christians, are the light of the world that separates the world from the darkness. What Jesus is saying is that we must not relent. We must not be quiet about our faith (being placed under a basket). We must be ambassadors for the kingdom of God. Jesus' brother James says it best below:

> *Be doers of the word, and not hearers only. Otherwise, you are deceiving yourselves. For anyone who hears the word but does not carry it out is like a man who looks at his face in a mirror, and after observing himself goes away and immediately forgets what he looks like. But the one who looks intently into the perfect law of freedom, and continues to do so—not being a forgetful hearer, but an effective doer—he will be blessed in what he does. (James 1:22-25)*

Wherever Christians walk, wherever they travel, the presence of God is there. Christians are bearers of light because God's Holy Spirit dwells inside of us. We should not let that light inside of us remain small or go out. We should rather nurture that light and allow it to grow and manifest in our daily lives.

Jesus Fulfilling the Law

"Do not think that I have come to abolish the Law or the Prophets. I have not come to abolish them, but to fulfill them. For I tell you truly, until heaven and earth pass away, not a single jot, not a stroke of a pen, will disappear from the Law until everything is accomplished.

So then, whoever breaks one of the least of these commandments and teaches others to do likewise will be called least in the kingdom of heaven; but whoever practices and teaches them will be called great in the kingdom of heaven. For I tell you that unless your righteousness exceeds that of the scribes and Pharisees, you will never enter the kingdom of heaven." (Matthew 5:17-20)

Jesus makes an important point here regarding Christians. Many Christians believe that only the New Testament applies. As mentioned earlier and to emphasize now, this is dangerous thinking. The entire Old Testament points to Jesus. That is why He came to fulfill and not abolish the law.

It is all about Jesus. Jesus fulfilled over 324 prophecies regarding the Messiah in the Old Testament.[14] The probability of a fraction of those prophecies being fulfilled by one person is

---

[14] Bernis, "How Many Messianic Prophecies Did Jesus Fulfill in Scripture?"

amazingly rare, especially by chance. The messiah is the only person who could have fulfilled over 324 prophecies, something truly impossible.

Jesus also mentions that heaven and earth won't pass away until everything is fulfilled in the Law. There are still prophecies in the Old Testament that haven't been fulfilled, including items also written in the Book of Revelation (which, of course, was written after Jesus' Death, Burial, and Resurrection). As one of our Christian duties, we must study and know the word. Some Christian circles would say to "be a Berean." Bereans diligently verified preached content to the scriptures to ensure truthfulness (ref Acts 17:10-11).

Jesus then goes into defining the penalty for leading people astray. If someone waters down God's word or teaches people the wrong things, they will be called least in the kingdom. If they fully adhere to the word of God and teach the entire Bible (not bits and pieces of what they believe), they will be called great in the kingdom of God.

Regarding righteousness, Jesus is calling Christians into a holy righteousness emanating from one's spirit. The Pharisees were righteous, but their heart posture was incorrect. The righteousness of the Pharisees and scribes was based on works and what they could do to earn God's approval. We should all try our hardest to gain God's approval. Without God's generous mercy and grace, one can't achieve salvation alone, and their self-righteous efforts are like filthy rags (see Isaiah 64:6).

Anger and Murder

"You have heard that it was said to the ancients, 'Do not murder' and 'Anyone who murders will be subject to judgment.' But I tell you that anyone who is angry with his brother will be subject to judgment. Again, anyone who says to his brother, 'Raca,' will be subject to the Sanhedrin. But anyone who says, 'You fool!' will be subject to the fire of hell.

So if you are offering your gift at the altar and there remember that your brother has something against you, leave your gift there before the altar. First go and be reconciled to your brother; then come and offer your gift.

Reconcile quickly with your adversary, while you are still on the way to court. Otherwise, he may hand you over to the judge, and the judge may hand you over to the officer, and you may be thrown into prison. Truly I tell you, you will not

get out until you have paid the last penny."
(Matthew 5:21-26)

Remember one of The Ten Commandments "Thou shall not murder," Jesus is revealing what the true intent behind that commandment was. He gives a pretty strict commandment in Matthew 5:22 stating that being angry with someone could subject you to judgment.

The virtue of yielding one's tongue has been taught for ages and was often mentioned in Proverbs. The word "Raca" means 'empty or empty-headed.'[15] NASB 95 translation calls "Raca" good-for-nothing. The word "Raca" today would be the same as calling someone worthless, trash, ghetto, or any other derogatory term; usually as racism or sexism or any way to make someone feel low of themselves (like hitting rock bottom). As per Jesus, what would this punishment be?

Being subject to the Sanhedrin, who are they? Merriam-Webster defines Sanhedrin as "the supreme council and tribunal of the Jews during post-exilic times headed by a High Priest and

---

[15] Strong, *The New Strong's Expanded Exhaustive Concordance of the Bible*.

having religious, civil, and criminal jurisdiction."[16] Imagine today in the USA, what could sound like common speech when people get angry, the applicable Supreme Court will try them when going to heaven. This concept further exemplifies the importance of watching what we say and how we say it. But yet there is more.

Jesus mentioned that when someone is called a fool, they will be thrown in hell. What? Children (and some adults) are bullied daily by others insulting their intelligence, looks, actions, etc. Maybe this is why many people get depressed and even resort to suicide. They get condemned by the world and get to a point of believing the lies and would rather die than live. I haven't been a direct eyewitness of this yet, but I have heard many testimonies of Christians telling a complete stranger what God thinks about or how God sees them and the stranger breaks out in a stream of tears. They were all stories of people going to kill themselves but gave society a chance for one more day. They didn't expect God to hear them and show up just in time. We must yield our tongues

---

[16] "Definition of SANHEDRIN."

in anger because we can do way more damage than we realize, especially if it is directed to those we have authority over (i.e. parent to child, teacher to student, etc.)

We no longer sacrifice animals, so what is Jesus talking about by leaving your offering? In the Old Covenant, animal sacrifice was how people would make atonement for their sins. Since Jesus has shed His precious blood on the cross and sealed us into the New Covenant, what could he be saying? Well, our altars are our prayer or alone time with God. If we are angry with someone and want to ask God for something; our anger will cause a block, no matter how harsh, loud, or charismatic we are with our words and actions in prayer. We must stop and pray for them first (always thinking of others first) or, better yet, settle the matter before our personal prayers can be heard.

Lastly, Jesus mentions we need to settle our affairs before it is too late. We need to attempt to settle matters the Biblical way instead of just letting things go. Letting things go is the way of the world and it doesn't work (I can personally testify to this). Heaven forbid something happens to us and we pass away. There will be no "Game Over" banner with a respawn/restart option; what is done is done, and we will have to pay for it in the end.

Adultery

"You have heard that it was said, 'Do not commit adultery.' But I tell you that anyone who looks at a woman to lust after her has already committed adultery with her in his heart. If your right eye causes you to sin, gouge it out and throw it away. It is better for you to lose one part of your body than for your whole body to be thrown into hell. And if your right hand causes you to sin, cut it off and throw it away. It is better for you to lose one part of your body than for your whole body to depart into hell." (Matthew 5:27-30)

Honesty, have you seen anyone pluck out their eye or cut off their hand, let alone willingly? Jesus isn't being literal here at all. His expressions here are what some would call an extreme hyperbole, and were common during that time. Jesus is just emphasizing His last sentence; it is better to lose a body part on the earth versus living in hell for an eternity.

Paralleling "Thou shall not murder," committing adultery follows suit. It isn't the very act of cheating on a spouse, thinking and desiring to be with another is the same as doing it. Jesus doesn't play around, does he? Such a high standard we must live by. But truly think about it, if you are married and your heart burns for another, isn't that going to cause problems in the marriage? I have seen marriages fall apart from moments of weakness. I know of people who have killed themselves (or tried) versus living with the shame and guilt of performing such an act. I also know many couples that have grown stronger because of an event (or ongoing event) of adultery. I also know some couples that are in the middle. In the end, God will deal with us and we shouldn't give in to the enemy. Some might say, "I'm saved; God will have grace on me to slip up once or twice; what's the harm?" Well, is that person really following God's word or bending the rules to suit themselves? We shouldn't walk on a tightrope; we should walk on that firm foundation in the Lord. It isn't worth falling into known unrepentant sin, and ultimately going to hell.

Divorce

"It has also been said, 'Whoever divorces his wife must give her a certificate of divorce.' But I tell you that anyone who divorces his wife, except for

sexual immorality, brings adultery upon her. And he who marries a divorced woman commits adultery." (Matthew 5:31-32)

The Law of Moses allowed for the people of Israel to be divorced by issuing a certificate of divorce. Moses established this in Deuteronomy 24:1-4. The original intent of this part of the law wasn't to promote divorce, it was to be presented as unnecessary except in extreme conditions. Jesus is taking this a step further to explain truly how one should live righteous and holy. Later, in Matthew Chapter 19, Jesus was asked further about divorce:

Then some Pharisees came and tested Him by asking, "Is it lawful for a man to divorce his wife for any reason?"

Jesus answered, "Have you not read that from the beginning the Creator 'made them male and female,' and said, 'For this reason a man will leave his father and mother and be united to his wife, and the two will become one flesh'? So they are no longer two, but one flesh. Therefore what God has joined together, let man not separate."

"Why then," they asked, "did Moses order a man to give his wife a certificate of divorce and send her away?"

Jesus replied, "Moses permitted you to divorce your wives because of your hardness of heart; but it was not this way from the beginning. Now I tell you that whoever divorces his wife, except for sexual immorality, and marries another woman, commits adultery." (Matthew 19:3-9)

Just like the Lord, Jesus didn't change his words and backed everything up with facts. The Lord created marriage for life, not for separation if times get tough. Per the Bible, divorce should only be because of sexual immorality (meaning the spouse committed adultery, more on adultery in the previous sub-section).

Making Oaths and Swearing

"Again, you have heard that it was said to the ancients, 'Do not break your oath, but fulfill your vows to the Lord.' But I tell you not to swear at all: either by heaven, for it is God's throne; or by the earth, for it is His footstool; or by Jerusalem, for it is the city of the great King. Nor should you swear by your head, for you cannot make a single hair white or black. Simply let your 'Yes' be 'Yes,' and your 'No,' 'No.' Anything more comes from the evil one." (Matthew 5:33-37)

Oaths spoken by the Hebrew people were common in those days. The issue is they would swear by the examples given by Jesus (swear by heaven, their heads, etc.). One common oath today is on a dead relative's grave, or on one's spouse, or on one's child or children. This can be dangerous because if the person giving the oath doesn't fulfill their part of the bargain, they have to pay up what is owed. As Jesus brings up, one can't swear by the earth, the moon, or whatever because it is not theirs or under their control. Just remember that if someone asks you to do something, be truthful. Let your "Yes" be "Yes" and your "No" be "No." If you will not do it or aren't sure, just say so. It would be better to be truthful than to lie to someone's face, especially if they trust you.

Retaliation and Being Generous

"You have heard that it was said, 'Eye for eye and tooth for tooth.' But I tell you not to resist an evil person. If someone slaps you on your right cheek, turn to him the other also; if someone wants to sue you and take your tunic, let him have your cloak as well; and if someone forces you to go one mile, go with him two miles. Give to the one who asks you, and do not turn away from the one who wants to borrow from you." (Matthew 5:38-42)

This book mentioned the "Eye for eye and tooth for tooth" earlier. The phrase is mentioned three times in the Old Testament and was used to describe different instances.

- Exodus 21:23-25 Deals with many issues relating to injuring others or their animals or their slaves. The information from this section of scripture is too much to briefly summarize (see Exodus 21:12-36 for the full description of all that was and wasn't allowed).

- Leviticus 24:19-20 Deals with what happens if someone injures or kills someone else or an animal, no matter if they were a foreigner or an Israelite.

- Deuteronomy 19:21 Deals with what happens if someone appears as a false witness or false accuser of brethren.

Jesus is telling the people that the above was not to be done in retaliation; the point is to live in a community with all people. Jesus is saying to give generously to those who are persecuting you. The nature of Christians is not to be frugal in everything, we should be a generous people. Jesus even says later in scripture that we should pray for our enemies (see Matthew 5:44-45). We are to help those in need, whether we know or dislike or love them. We shouldn't be generous because of clout or to be noticed. That is something the

Pharisees would have done during the time of the New Testament. When was the last time you helped your neighbor? What about that old, widowed lady down the street? What about that random person with a flat tire? What about that person who just spit in your face? What? Why would I do that? They hate me. Maybe they don't really know you, or you know them. Perhaps they have never experienced the heart of the Lord. Use those times to truly shine as a Christian and not retaliate against those who dislike you. If you get in the way and you retaliate, you will be seen as everyone else in the world. Act as God's chosen people, be set apart, and endure with humility.

More on Generosity

"Be careful not to perform your righteous acts before men to be seen by them. If you do, you will have no reward from your Father in heaven.

So when you give to the needy, do not sound a trumpet before you, as the hypocrites do in the synagogues and on the streets, to be honored by men. Truly I tell you, they already have their full reward. But when you give to the needy, do not let your left hand know what your right hand is doing, so that your giving may be in secret. And your Father, who sees what is done in secret, will reward you." (Matthew 6:1-4)

Isn't it funny how Jesus explained "Do not sound a trumpet before you" when giving to the poor? Imagine if Rodney Dangerfield's car horn from the movie Caddyshack would go off every time someone gave to the poor. That would surely be a sight to see. On a serious note, the people who are either homeless or panhandling are doing it for a reason and are indeed in need. Now, there are some that take advantage of people's generosity, but when you think about it, they have to answer to the Lord for that. I met a good friend by stopping to help and speak to him while he was panhandling. We prayed together and all glory to God, he got healed in his legs (he could barely walk and was resting when I stopped to talk to him). We still talk to this day and are helping each other grow. Why do I mention this? Generosity and kindness can change lives and alter the path we are on. When was the last time you stopped to help someone who needed a ride or some money to buy food? Do you have a poor neighbor who can't work or is older and widowed? If so, when was the last time you offered to do yard work for them so they could stretch their money a little more? This is the kindness Jesus is talking about, not on public display; it can be anywhere (i.e., someone's house or porch, work cubicle, grocery store aisle, etc.). I feel led to mention that blessings come through obedience and discipline. As a friend of mine says in some of his teachings on spiritual and physical disciplines, "It matters most when no one is looking" to show your maturity in the Lord. Living a disciplined life as a Christian is most important.

Jesus on Prayer

"Also, when you pray, do not be like the hypocrites; for they love to pray [publicly] standing in the synagogues and on the corners of the streets so that they may be seen by men. I assure you and most solemnly say to you, they [already] have their reward in full. But when you pray, go into your most private room, close the door and pray to your Father who is in secret, and your Father who sees [what is done] in secret will reward you.

"And when you pray, do not use meaningless repetition as the Gentiles do, for they think they will be heard because of their many words. So do not be like them [praying as they do]; for your Father knows what you need before you ask Him.

"Pray, then, in this way:

'Our Father, who is in heaven, Hallowed be Your name. Your kingdom come, Your will be done On earth as it is in heaven. Give us this day our daily

bread. And forgive us our debts, as we have forgiven our debtors [letting go of both the wrong and the resentment]. And do not lead us into temptation, but deliver us from evil. [For Yours is the kingdom and the power and the glory forever. Amen.]'

For if you forgive others their trespasses [their reckless and willful sins], your heavenly Father will also forgive you. But if you do not forgive others [nurturing your hurt and anger with the result that it interferes with your relationship with God], then your Father will not forgive your trespasses. (Matthew 6:5-15 AMP)

Prayer is a lifeline for Christians. Jesus gives us the basics.

Rule #1: Don't pray just to be seen by all or for popularity. Always seek God in secret. Does this mean that you can't pray for someone in public? Nope, praying for someone in public is acceptable. If one is doing it not to be seen, coming from a place of love and compassion for the people, that is acceptable each and every day of the week. Seeking in secret just means not to make a public display of yourself. Of course, we should pray and pray often. A life of prayerlessness is detrimental in Christianity. If you stop talking to someone, do you honestly think they will want to communicate with you? Prayer is our communication with God.

If we stop talking to God, He will not want to talk to us.

Rule #2: Do not babble. Jesus means do not chant or be super repetitive. In pagan religions and certain types of witchcraft, they say chants as a form of prayer to what is being prayed to. Prayer with God should be a two-way conversation, not just a three-to-five-minute session of only you talking to God and then you are done.

Jesus broke down the template of prayer into sections (in the following order):

1. [Our Father...] Glorify God and the Father and declare His sovereignty.

2. [Give us this...] Being thankful and asking for our daily provision.

3. [And forgive us...] Forgive our sins and those that have sinned against us.

4. [And lead us not...] God doesn't tempt us (the enemy does), He puts us through trials that can expose us to the enemy (if we so choose).

5. [For yours is the kingdom and the power and the glory forever. Amen.] Some translations exclude this, but this section of the verse is more for us to remember the sovereignty of God.

At the end of the prayer, Jesus broke down further the importance of forgiveness. If we forgive others for the wrong things done to us, we ourselves will be forgiven. But, if we hold on to the wrongs and have unforgiveness, ours will not be forgiven. A common theme in the New Testament and this book is love for one another. Through all that Jesus and others in the New Testament teach, love is everything. The highest form of love, Agape, is what each and every Christian should have toward everyone. If this weren't the case, Jesus wouldn't have said so in John 13:35. Just remember, if we don't forgive out of love for others, we should really examine ourselves to ensure we aren't walking in error.

Finally, I want to stress that with prayer; it is about the quality and quantity of time spent with God. If someone can only pray for a few minutes and then give up, that is okay. It is like learning how to ride a bicycle or playing a new video game. Just keep trying. With prayer, we need to keep in mind that God is our heavenly Father. He will never leave us, nor forsake us (see Deuteronomy 31:6). God wants to spend time with us. We are His children. I want all of us to reflect on where we spend a lot of our extra time? Is it a hobby? A new video game? Binge-watching YouTube or a favorite series of shows or movies? How would you feel if your children did the same and only spoke to you for 3-5 minutes each day? The more time we spend in His presence, the easier it is to hear and know His voice. Jesus used to slip away to spend time alone in prayer for long periods of time. Since Jesus is our perfect example, shouldn't we do the same?

Fasting

"When you fast, do not be somber like the hypocrites, for they disfigure their faces to show men they are fasting. Truly I tell you, they already have their full reward. But when you fast, anoint your head and wash your face, so that your fasting will not be obvious to men, but only to your Father, who is unseen. And your Father, who sees what is done in secret, will reward you." (Matthew 6:16-18)

Fasting. This is a big debate in most modern-day churches. Let's point out the biggest deciding factor, the first three words: "WHEN YOU FAST!" Wow, that is pretty straightforward! Since we are still supposed to be fasting, now what? Don't disfigure your face while fasting. Okay, so act as you would normally and do nothing to alter your appearance. When we fast, we are to shower and do all the normal things so no one is aware of what we are doing. The Pharisees would make themselves look dirty or paler than normal, or wear certain clothes during fasts. They did this to be noticed by everyone else. They wanted to be seen to prove their righteousness and devotion toward God to others.

What isn't mentioned above is there are different types of fasting. The most common is fasting from food or certain types of foods. Another would be too fast from television, social media, electronics, hobbies, etc. to focus on the Lord. Fasts can be long or short. Sometimes, the Lord will lead you into a specific fast; other times, a fast can come from us as a dedication to the Lord. In Luke, the Pharisees mention they fast twice a week (see Luke 18:12). The problem is that they were self-righteous and believed that doing things for the Lord would earn their way to heaven. If you truly devote a fast to the Lord, be disciplined and intentional. Ensure you spend that extra time in prayer and the Word. Remember, the Lord sees what is done in secret and will reward you. There are several examples of people fasting for specific reasons in the Old Testament.

Where is your Treasure?

"Do not store up for yourselves treasures on earth, where moth and rust destroy, and where thieves break in and steal. But store up for yourselves treasures in heaven, where moth and rust do not destroy, and where thieves do not break in and steal. For where your treasure is, there your heart will be also." (Matthew 6:19-21)

Jesus gives a proclamation on wealth, true wealth. True wealth is being spiritually rich. What does it mean to be spiritually rich? In the world, one that is rich likes to invest their money wisely. Wise investments can take some time and planning. The investments can be physical assets (i.e. paintings, cars, businesses, properties, etc.) or money or precious metals. Investments in the spiritual is spending time with the Lord, prayer, reading/studying the Bible, and more. The more one can glean from the teachings of Jesus and the Bible (Word of God), the greater the investment into the treasures of heaven.

Jesus doesn't dislike someone for being wealthy. The Bible in many places teaches about how to be

Walking with God: Exploring Creation, Fall of Man, Laws, and Faith

good stewards of money. What is being said is don't let being wealthy or loving money consume your life. Look up the endless stories of people coming into money, winning millions in the lottery, or becoming famous. Either they go bankrupt within a certain timeframe or become completely miserable. Living in misery isn't from God. Take some time to review and reflect on the last sentence "For where your treasure is, there your heart will be also." So ...What do you treasure most? Remember the first commandment. Perhaps there is a link between it and this portion of Jesus' teaching. Let us always look to God first and foremost, He will never lead us astray.

God Will Provide

Therefore I tell you, do not worry about your life, what you will eat or drink; or about your body, what you will wear. Is not life more than food, and the body more than clothes? Look at the birds of the air: They do not sow or reap or gather into barns—and yet your heavenly Father feeds them. Are you not much more valuable than they? Who of you by worrying can add a single hour to his life?

And why do you worry about clothes? Consider how the lilies of the field grow: They do not labor or spin. Yet I tell you that not even Solomon in all his glory was adorned like one of these. If that is how God clothes the grass of the field, which is here today and tomorrow is thrown into the furnace, will He not much more clothe you, O you of little faith?

Therefore do not worry, saying, 'What shall we eat?' or 'What shall we drink?' or 'What shall we wear?' For the Gentiles strive after all these things, and your heavenly Father knows that you need them. But seek first the kingdom of God and His righteousness, and all these things will be added unto you.

Therefore do not worry about tomorrow, for tomorrow will worry about itself. Today has enough trouble of its own. (Matthew 6:25-34)

Do not worry about your life or your body. Do not worry about what you will eat, drink, and wear. God is a God of provision and abundance. God can part the Red Sea and allow His people to cross it on dry land. He provided manna from heaven in the wilderness, water from a rock, and so on. If we are faithful, He will take care of us. I know of countless stories where God provided for many people on more than one occasion, including my family. Should we all just up and quit our jobs to let God provide for all of us? Well, if God didn't tell you to do so, I wouldn't suggest it. I know people who have every need met by God daily, but you see, they were called into that position by the Lord. If we aren't called, we are acting in disobedience.

Who of you, by worrying, can add a single hour to your life? If we worry about everything or have to work our tails off to get that nice car or a big house or whatever, what are we really trusting in? Is it in what we want or are we trusting in and resting in God? If we are in God's rest, we will be unshakable. "Seek first the kingdom and all will be added" is a popular scripture modern day Christians use (notice they forget to mention His righteousness). This verse is not a one-liner to get what you want; Jesus is saying again to rest in God and let His perfect peace be instilled in you.

The last sentence is another parallel to the other portions of the mentioned scripture. Don't worry about tomorrow. Rest in God's ever-loving arms and just let all your worries be carried away.

Judging Others

"Do not judge, or you will be judged. For with the same judgment you pronounce, you will be judged; and with the measure you use, it will be measured to you. Why do you look at the speck in your brother's eye, but fail to notice the beam in

your own eye? How can you say to your brother, 'Let me take the speck out of your eye,' while there is still a beam in your own eye? You hypocrite! First take the beam out of your own eye, and then you will see clearly to remove the speck from your brother's eye. Do not give dogs what is holy; do not throw your pearls before swine. If you do, they may trample them under their feet, and then turn and tear you to pieces." (Matthew 7:1-6)

We all need to watch our words and what we say. Jesus presents a good warning to the entire body of Christ. Many leaders and pastors have been exposed or have fallen into some sort of sin. We must not gossip about and slander their name(s), or we will be judged for the same thing. The entire Bible is packed full of God's love for His people (those who choose to follow Him) and creation (all of humanity). If we aren't operating out of a place of love, then we are operating out of the wrong spirit and with the wrong motives. Many are quick to speak and judge their neighbor when they are in the same sin themselves. Many people that operate not in the kingdom of God are doing so because of observance of this very thing fellow Christians operate in quite often. I know many people who have fallen away from the church for this reason. If we are doing the wrong things during the week and preaching against it on Sundays, that beam is still there, folks. Until we purge ourselves of all darkness and sin (yes, it takes work on our part), our lights can't shine brightly (remember, we are the Light of the World). Let us not be hypocrites like the Pharisees and Sadducees were. If we allow darkness to remain, that is like throwing your pearls before swine. It will consume you (tear you to pieces). Let God's light inside of you shine so brightly that all the darkness has to flee.

The Golden Rule

"In everything, then, do to others as you would have them do to you. For this is the essence of the Law and the Prophets." (Matthew 7:12)

The verse above is the golden rule of the entire Bible. It is what the classic "Eye for an Eye" comes from. The entire essence is to be acting from a place of love. If God had no love and forgiveness and mercy for His people, we would all be wiped off the face of the earth. Jesus would be the only one worthy to walk the earth if God had no love, forgiveness, and mercy. Some may say that God is merciless and all brimstone and fire. That is what I always thought. The more I dig into the word, look at God's position and where his heart is, He is truly a loving God and puts up with a lot of foolishness. Yes, there is a lot of killing and other things in the Old Testament, but God warned and warned the people, and they didn't listen. With Jesus as our example, rabbi (teacher), high priest, Lord, and savior, we need to use Him as an example to live by.

Seeking the Lord

"Ask, and it will be given to you; seek, and you will find; knock, and the door will be opened to you. For everyone who asks receives; he who seeks finds; and to him who knocks, the door will be opened. Which of you, if his son asks for bread, will give him a stone? Or if he asks for a fish, will give him a snake? So if you who are evil know how to give good gifts to your children, how much more will your Father in heaven give good things to those who ask Him!" (Matthew 7:7-11)

Have you ever played hide and seek? Holistically, many don't realize how available God is. As mentioned before, God is always in abundance, and His supply has no end. No one can outdo or outgive God, so what is this seek business? God wants you to seek Him desperately. If one diligently seeks after God, especially if being

143

pulled, God will find you. Jesus says that, "the door will be opened to you." Wait, did Jesus say "someone special" or "who I choose?" No Way! Jesus is talking about and to every person who heard or read the words He spoke.

What is all the gift stuff about? Well, God knows exactly what you need before asking for it (see Matthew 6:8). A gift is given and not taken back. God supplies every one of us with unique gifts depending on the grace that is in our lives. The most important thing is not the gifts but the seeking. Always seek God first, and He will ensure you always have what you need when you need it. We might not always see things in this manner, but as time goes on, reliance on Him will start teaching you otherwise.

The Wide and Narrow Gate

"Enter through the narrow gate. For wide is the gate and broad is the way that leads to destruction, and many enter through it. But small is the gate and narrow the way that leads to life, and only a few find it." (Matthew 7:13-14)

The two ways of life, the narrow or the broad/wide gate, are vastly different. The wide gate, of course, is a life of sin, deception, greed, living for the world and self, and being separated from God.

The term "pick your poison" comes to mind regarding living in the world. When living in and of the world, you are picking what is slowly killing you when not choosing God. In some seasons, one would consume more poison than during others, but it is still poison. The point is, we should all turn to God for forgiveness and choose to follow Him.

The narrow gate is a life in God that does not lead to destruction. Why wouldn't we seek the Lord and find the narrow gate? Wouldn't it be easier to draw a straight line versus trying to find the end of a large maze? The straight line will always let you know where you are going. The maze is always leading one into the unknown, confusion, worry, fear, and anxiety. Choosing God and His ways and living for Him gives one that simplistic method of knowing where to go and where that going will lead you. Remember not to go to the left or to the right; just keep straight on the path, and you can't go wrong.

Beware of False Prophets

"Beware of false prophets. They come to you in sheep's clothing, but inwardly they are ravenous wolves. By their fruit you will recognize them. Are grapes gathered from thornbushes, or figs from thistles? Likewise, every good tree bears good fruit, but a bad tree bears bad fruit. A good tree cannot bear bad fruit, and a bad tree cannot bear good fruit. Every tree that does not bear good fruit is cut down and thrown into the fire. So then, by their fruit you will recognize them." (Matthew 7:15-20)

False teachers and prophets have been around since the days of Noah. False prophets were also common during the life of Jesus. The Bible mentions being aware of the false prophets in both the Old and New Testaments. Let's look at what Jesus is telling us:

- They will seem harmless, but truly are there to lead people astray,

- Their fruit will be obvious. They will be leading people to themselves and not toward God or Jesus.

The Bible uses references to fruit many times in the New Testament. The basic premise with false prophets is to watch to see what the outcome of their actions is. Are they promoting something different from what is written in the Bible, even slightly different? Sounds kind of familiar, like the serpent in the garden of Eden or Satan with Jesus in the wilderness. Be prepared! The enemy can and will know the word of God. They twist scriptures, and people will buy into them and run to them. This completely blinds people who can't discern the truth from what tickles their ears. The Bible states the Lord said to one of His prophets, "My people perish for lack of knowledge" (see Hosea 4:6). In the end, God will throw them in the Lake of Fire for what they have done on the Earth. If they know the words in the Bible, they are also very aware of the warnings.

One question that could be asked is "How do you spot a false prophet" or a false teacher? The two points mentioned above will be a good start. It could be really hard if they are very charismatic. Holy Spirit should tell you by a quickening in your spirit or using a similar method. Some use discernment, but that could still be tricky. One good way is to take good notes and verify what they say with scripture. Every crossed "t" and dotted "i" are important in the Bible, so be like a Berean and study the word to show yourself

147

approved unto God (see 2 Timothy 2:15). If what they say and preach doesn't align with scripture, that is a good tell-tell sign that you have a false prophet or false teacher on your hands.

The True Way into the Kingdom

"Not everyone who says to Me, 'Lord, Lord,' will enter the kingdom of heaven, but only he who does the will of My Father in heaven. Many will say to Me on that day, 'Lord, Lord, did we not prophesy in Your name, and in Your name drive out demons and perform many miracles?' Then I will tell them plainly, 'I never knew you; depart from Me, you workers of lawlessness!'" (Matthew 7:21-23)

The only way into the kingdom is to do the will of the Lord. The three verses above should be on all our minds consistently. It is definitely on my mind daily. We must examine ourselves daily. Why are certain thoughts coming to our minds? Are we operating in the perfect will of God? People can be very charismatic, prophetic, and walking in the gifts of the spirit, but what is their heart's posture? Are they leading people astray (as mentioned above regarding false prophets)? Jesus is giving us perfect examples of the litmus test to see if we are walking in error or not. Jesus is also stating what will happen if we are walking in error.

We should be cautious to ensure we are fully walking in the spirit.

Foundation Building

"Therefore everyone who hears these words of Mine and acts on them is like a wise man who built his house on the rock. The rain fell, the torrents raged, and the winds blew and beat against that house; yet it did not fall, because its foundation was on the rock. But everyone who hears these words of Mine and does not act on them is like a foolish man who built his house on sand. The rain fell, the torrents raged, and the winds blew and beat against that house, and it fell—and great was its collapse!" (Matthew 7:24-27)

Time for the grand finale of the famous Sermon on the Mount. For those who don't know what a foundation is, foundations are what is put in place before one builds on it. A common house in the USA can have a stone, concrete block, concrete slab, buried wooden piers, etc. depending on where it is being built. Skyscrapers require a very big and deep foundation to offset the weight and height of the building. Roads have base layers that are used as a foundation for the top layers of asphalt or concrete or gravel. Our foundation could be how we were raised (poor, middle class, wealthy, etc.) and what we learned as children (through school, churches, friends, acquaintances, workplaces, mentors, teachers, managers, etc.). Everyone and everything have some kind of foundation. The big question Jesus is asking the people is, what kind of foundation are you built upon? Over time, our foundations need amounts of maintenance, repair, and, in certain instances, replacement.

The people attending this wonderful sermon were living under the Law of Moses. They also didn't have access to the Holy Spirit yet. They were still living in a fallen world riddled with sin, and, as mentioned earlier, the Law of Moses was to show a way for the people to be forgiven of their sins. Why all this explanation? Well, the people of that day only knew the word of God by what was shared during the temple services. As Jesus mentioned, He came to fulfill the law and not abolish it. All that Jesus preached in the four gospels should be taken into much consideration by each believer. After all, Jesus is our perfect example of how we are to walk, live, and breathe on this earth. Building our life's foundation on the teachings of Jesus is most definitely a foundation built on the rock. A foundation built on sand is living for this world, for ourselves, for the satisfaction of our flesh, aimlessly chasing riches and fame, and all the like. Please read through and absorb the words of King Solomon in the book of Proverbs. What Jesus taught will not interfere with the words of King Solomon, the wisest king that had ever lived. Now is a good time to reflect upon our lives. What foundation are you built on? Is it the rock or the sand?

Sermon on the Mount vs The Ten Commandments

Jesus' Sermon on the Mount is powerful, but is not a totality of all of His teachings. As mentioned earlier, some topics preached overlaps with the Ten Commandments. God gave the Ten Commandments to the Hebrew people at Mount Sinai. It would make perfect sense the Messiah would also teach and confirm what God gave to His chosen people. The author has put together a table below as a reference to the reader. The section titles match the sections in this volume. Please refer to each appropriate section and any further study resources to dive deeper into any of the covered sections and topics.

	Ten Commandments	Sermon on the Mount
1	Shall have no other gods before God.	• Jesus on Prayer • Where is Your Treasure?
2	Shall not make for yourself an idol.	• Beware of False Prophets
3	Shall not take the name of the LORD your God in vain.	• Making Oaths and Swearing
4	Remember the Sabbath day by keeping it holy.	• Seeking the Lord
5	Honor your father and mother.	• Jesus on Prayer
6	You shall not murder.	• Anger and Murder
7	You shall not commit adultery.	• Adultery • Divorce
8	You shall not steal.	• God Will Provide
9	You shall not bear false witness against your neighbor.	• Judging Others
10	You shall not covet anything owned by your neighbor.	• Adultery

Figure 1: Ten Commandments and Sermon on the Mount Reference Table

Concluding Thoughts

Jesus' Sermon on the Mount is one of the most powerful sermons in the Bible. He covers almost all aspects of the Christian life. After this sermon, or even each section of this sermon, we should all have a "selah" moment (moment of thought and reflection). Jesus unpacks a powerful teaching covering multiple aspects of what we should all do and not do. I pray the tie-in with the Ten Commandments and items Jesus spoke about in the sermon takes root. God established everything out of love for His creation. Jesus came to fulfill the Law of Moses, not abolish it. Everything in the Bible ties together and is for every believer. We can't pick and choose what parts we want to believe in the Bible. It completely applies to all Christians.

Practical Application

Jesus himself states that He is here to fulfill the Law, not abolish it. With this truth, we all should rest assured that all does apply. The material covered is just a tiny portion of the New Testament. Systemically breaking everything down in the New Testament would take many volumes of books, just like this one. Regarding the Sermon on the Mount preached by Jesus, the following could apply to any believer:

- Many blessings are available to all Christians that walk as Jesus has described in the Beatitudes. Carefully review to see what areas of your life that needs improvement.

- Don't lose your saltiness. Always be in a place of self-examination and self-improvement.

- Die to yourself daily so that God can work through you.

- Be "The Light of the World" by being ambassadors of the Kingdom of Heaven.

- All believers should be led toward Jesus, no excuses.

- The entire Bible points to Jesus. If someone is teaching a different doctrine, fact check them and study to find yourself approved.

- Be cautious of false teachers and false prophets that glorify themselves.

- Do not even think of murder or adultery or you will be guilty of performing that sin in the eyes of the Lord.

- If you have something against someone, even your enemies, reconcile it before doing anything else.

- Retaliation is not a trait of a Christian.

- The Lord does not accept divorce unless the spouse commits adultery.

- Do not swear or make oaths. Agree or disagree, and move on.

- Generosity and kindness go a long way, make it a lifestyle. Generosity relates to time, talent, or money. Being kind and helping a stranger or a neighbor can go a long way.

- Prayer is a Christian's lifeline. That is how we talk to God. Jesus gave us a basic template for prayer.

- Jesus reminds us to forgive others so that we will be forgiven of our sins.

- Fasting is still a requirement for all Christians.

- Focus on being spiritually rich. Spend time with God in prayer and in the word.

155

- God doesn't care if someone is poor or wealthy.

- God cares about one's heart posture. Is it toward Him or greed and malice?

- Worrying is not a fruitful trait. Resting in the peace of God is the best place to be.

- We should all come from a place of love with everything we do and speak.

- Do not judge others, do not gossip.

- Keep seeking the Lord, enter the narrow gate, and stay on the straight and narrow path.

- Always, always, always ensure one is being pointed to Jesus and NOT a man or anything or anyone else.

- Ensure one has a deep foundation built on God. If the earth shakes, will it collapse? Sooner or later, things will become shaken.

CHAPTER 7

---◄○►---

Introduction to Faith

Faith, as mentioned earlier in the section covering Spiritual Laws, is like fuel in the kingdom of God. Faith is one of the most important practices Christians need to practice and live by. Faith is so powerful; Jesus made an emphasis on faith and what it can do.

"Because you have so little faith," He answered. "For truly I tell you, if you have faith the size of a mustard seed, you can say to this mountain, 'Move from here to there,' and it will move. Nothing will be impossible for you." (Matthew 17:20)

And the Lord answered, "If you have faith the size of a mustard seed, you can say to this mulberry tree, 'Be uprooted and planted in the sea,' and it will obey you. (Luke 17:6)

Faith the size of a mustard seed. Do you know how big a mustard seed is? Well, it is pretty small. If a person has a small amount of faith and can metaphorically move mountains, what can happen if one has a large amount of faith? Examine yourself at the end of this book and ask yourself, "How much faith do I have?" Now that we have a brief introduction to faith and its power, let us look at the definition of the word. Merriam-Webster defines 'Faith' as:

allegiance to duty or a person (i.e. loyalty)

fidelity to one's promises

sincerity of intentions

belief and trust in and loyalty to God

belief in the traditional doctrines of a religion

firm belief in something for which there is no proof

complete trust

something that is believed, especially with strong conviction[17]

---

[17] "Definition of FAITH."

Thomas Nelson in The New Strong's Expanded Exhaustive Concordance of the Bible, defines Faith and Faithfulness as:

- Faith: confidence in the testimony of another.[18]
- Faithfulness: making faith a living reality in one's life.[19]

Faith is truly one of the hardest things for someone to grasp and implement in their life. It is very interesting to see how the word faith is used in the Bible. Per 'The New Strong's Expanded Exhaustive Concordance of the Bible,' the KJV uses the word "Faith" only twice in the Old Testament; compared to two hundred forty-five times in the New Testament.[20] We won't cover every one of them. Let us start with what the Bible says about faith in the Old Testament.

He said: "I will hide My face from them; I will see what will be their end.

For they are a perverse generation—children of unfaithfulness. (Deuteronomy 32:20)

---

[18] Strong, *The New Strong's Expanded Exhaustive Concordance of the Bible.*

[19] Strong.

[20] Strong.

In this passage, God is speaking to Moses. The people of Israel were rescued out of slavery from the Land of Egypt. Now, they have turned away from God to pursue idols and unknown gods and have made God jealous and very angry. Deuteronomy Chapter 32 is a wonderful chapter to read on how God is toward people that turn away from Him. God decided to pour His anger out on them. In the end, the people of Israel couldn't enter the promised land until the generation of people that fled Egypt died. What would have been a couple weeks' journey through the wilderness to the promised land took forty years and death to a generation because of disobedience. I hope this shows what happens when faith isn't in the picture. I assure you, being in the wilderness isn't a place you want to be.

> *Look at the proud one; his soul is not upright but the righteous will live by faith and wealth indeed betrays him. He is an arrogant man never at rest. He enlarges his appetite like Sheol, and like Death, he is never satisfied. He gathers all the nations to himself and collects all the peoples as his own. (Habakkuk 2:4-5)*

In this passage, the Lord reveals that the proud, the rich, and the leaders of the people are acting out of the wrong spirit. They were going after fame, power, and lust to glorify themselves. Then God mentions, 'The just shall live by faith.' The just are the people who follow God's statutes and reverence Him, His chosen people. I believe this applies to then and now. Jesus mentions in the New Testament:

In His teaching Jesus also said, "Watch out for the scribes. They like to walk around in long robes, to receive greetings in the marketplaces, and to have the chief seats in the synagogues and the places of honor at banquets. They defraud widows of their houses, and for a show make lengthy prayers. These men will receive greater condemnation."

As Jesus was sitting opposite the treasury, He watched the crowd putting money into it. And many rich people put in large amounts. Then one poor widow came and put in two small copper coins, which amounted to a small fraction of a denarius.

Jesus called His disciples to Him and said, "Truly I tell you, this poor widow has put more than all the others into the treasury. For they all contributed out of their surplus, but she out of her poverty has put in all she had to live on." *(Mark 12:38-44)*

Jesus is giving a good parallel to Habakkuk 2:4 in the above. The scribes loved having all the fine clothes and prestigious rank in society. The

161

scribes had puffed up souls but were missing the boat regarding faith and living by the word of God. In the above passages, the rich people showed up at the temple and would bring in bags of money and give to be seen. It was probably often that they would boast or try to outdo one another. People nowadays want the latest phones, gadgets, computers, vehicles, etc. Does that all sound familiar (without donating to a temple or church)? I remember the big race of who could build the best computer rig to harvest the most packets in folding. This is all the same thing: PRIDE! Nothing stops faith from working like pride. We must put ourselves aside and look at the one who redeemed us from eternal damnation.

Moving on to the poor widow that gave the two mites (some translations say copper coins), basically two pennies, two-pence, two kronor, etc., to live on. Why did she give all that she had? She knew God would take care of her. The poor widow had true, genuine faith. She gave God her whole heart in adoration, not just a piece of it. If you have ever been at rock bottom and trusted in God to pull you out, and sure enough, He did, that builds true rock-solid faith. I am not saying to spend or give away all you have and trust that it will be replenished. I am saying that God will take care of those that love Him. I can testify that sometimes those who don't know God all that well will be taken care of. When you trust our Heavenly Father with all things, you can't go wrong.

Concluding Thoughts

It is essential to establish an understanding of what faith is and is not. We need to grasp basic knowledge before moving forward to the later sections of this book.

Practical Application

Faith might seem like a simple concept to grasp. I have experienced people not wholly grasping this concept. It might seem easy for seasoned believers, but at different times, all believers struggle with their faith. God is looking for a pure heart that puts it all in for Him. Look at the example of the poor widow who gave the two coins. It wasn't the fact that she gave all the money she had; it was the fact that she gave God her all and fully trusted Him. She knew that no matter what, God would take care of her. We should all do a daily faith check on ourselves. Where do you stand?

CHAPTER 8

Jesus on Faith

Jesus is the best example we have regarding learning about the kingdom of Heaven. Since we have just gone through a brief overview of faith, let us dive deeper into the subject.

When Jesus had entered Capernaum, a centurion came and pleaded with Him, "Lord, my servant lies at home, paralyzed and in terrible agony."

"I will go and heal him," Jesus replied.

The centurion answered, "Lord, I am not worthy to have You come under my roof. But just say the word, and my servant will be healed. For I myself am a man under authority, with soldiers under me. I tell one to go, and he goes; and another to come, and he comes. I tell my servant to do something, and he does it."

When Jesus heard this, He marveled and said to those following Him, "Truly I tell you, I have not found anyone in Israel with such great faith. I say to you that many will come from the east and the west to share the banquet with Abraham, Isaac, and Jacob in the kingdom of heaven. But the sons of the kingdom will be thrown into the outer darkness, where there will be weeping and gnashing of teeth."

Then Jesus said to the centurion, "Go! As you have believed, so will it be done for you." And his servant was healed at that very hour. (Matthew 8:5-13)

The passage above discusses a Roman centurion who believed 100% that Jesus would heal his servant. The centurions were renowned men of high regard and were greatly respected. As mentioned, they commanded large amounts of people in the Roman army. It was an honor for Jesus to visit the centurion's house. However, the centurion said he wasn't worthy to have Jesus visit his house because of his status. He believed Jesus needed only to speak the word, and it would be done. The centurion believed that Jesus' words would be sufficient because of his faith. The faith of the centurion was so great that Jesus commended him of it to the disciples. Imagine this, God incarnate that was physically walking the earth "Marveled" at the centurion's faith. The other important thing to realize is that Roman centurions were also probably pagan and worshipped the various Roman gods, but this centurion believed Jesus could speak and his servant would be healed. How can the high status, high net-worth to the below poverty level population of today see the same take place in their lives? Simply, do what the centurion did, place your faith in Jesus, and rest in that decision. If you are following the Lord and living the proper way, He will always come through.

Faith and Prayer

"Truly I tell you," Jesus replied, "if you have faith and do not doubt, not only will you do what was done to the fig tree, but even if you say to this mountain, 'Be lifted up and thrown into the sea,' it will happen. If you believe, you will receive whatever you ask for in prayer." (Matthew 21:21-22)

Again, Jesus is giving us part of the perfect equation for prayer. Ask in faith and believe that you shall receive, and it shall be done. "Shall" might not be a popular term for some, but it simply means that it will happen. Once again, Jesus is giving us powerful advice on how to pray and what our stance needs to be to get things accomplished. No mountain is too high, nor any valley too low for the God of the Universe.

Resting Through the Storm

When He got into the boat, His disciples followed Him. Suddenly a violent storm came up on the sea, so that the boat was engulfed by the waves; but Jesus was sleeping. The disciples went and woke Him, saying, "Lord, save us! We are perishing!"

"You of little faith," Jesus replied, "why are you so afraid?" Then He got up and rebuked the winds and the sea, and it was perfectly calm.

The men were amazed and asked, "What kind of man is this? Even the winds and the sea obey Him!" (Matthew 8:23-27)

The point of the above passage isn't about controlling weather patterns. The disciples were in a great storm, imagine very rough waves and high winds. They were genuinely scared that they would lose their lives. What was Jesus doing? He was asleep. Jesus had peace in the storm. Our faith should root us into the fruits of the spirit and be able to give us reassurance that no matter what happens, we are safe and secure. How many great storms have you been through and truly relied on God and He came through? We should be continually thankful for those times.

Cleansing the Ten Lepers

As He entered one of the villages, He was met by ten lepers. They stood at a distance and raised their voices, shouting, "Jesus, Master, have mercy on us!"

When Jesus saw them, He said, "Go, show yourselves to the priests." And as they were on their way, they were cleansed.

When one of them saw that he was healed, he came back, praising God in a loud voice. He fell facedown at Jesus' feet in thanksgiving to Him— and he was a Samaritan.

"Were not all ten cleansed?" Jesus asked. "Where then are the other nine? Was no one found except this foreigner to return and give glory to God?"

Then Jesus said to him, "Rise and go; your faith has made you well!" (Luke 17:12-19)

To build off the ultimate point of thankfulness, the above passages are very important. Jesus healed ten lepers and sent them to the priests to declare that they are healed. The significance of this is that they could return to normal life, see their family and friends, and attend temple

169

services. The one key Jesus reveals is that only one returned to worship him, and a Samaritan at that. Samaritans didn't like the Jews (that is why the Good Samaritan parable is such a powerful example). Only one out of the ten healed stayed to worship God. Think about that, if ten people are saved of their sins and are no longer cast out of where they want to be, only one will stay to truly worship God for what He has done in their lives. If one of ten people who are saved are true worshippers of God and are truly thankful and will live for him, where do you stand? The better question would be, where do you want to stand? We all have the choice to choose who and what we serve. God has made it pretty plain and clear on what we should and shouldn't do. It is our choice to walk the walk. If you are already there, outstanding! If you aren't but want to be there, there is no better time than now to start. Rebuild your faith, repent and turn back to God and let him lead you.

Jesus Heals Two Blind Men

As Jesus went on from there, two blind men followed Him, crying out, "Have mercy on us, Son of David!"

After Jesus had entered the house, the blind men came to Him. "Do you believe that I am able to do this?" He asked.

"Yes, Lord," they answered.

Then He touched their eyes and said, "According to your faith will it be done to you." And their eyes were opened. Jesus warned them sternly, "See that no one finds out about this!" (Matthew 9:27-30)

In the above passages, Jesus healed two blind men. They were crying out to him for help to make them whole. Imagine what it would be like to be blind, especially in the time of Jesus. I couldn't begin to empathize, but I can imagine that one would feel pretty helpless. Then, Jesus came on the scene, and they were healed, and their sight was restored. Once we are truly healed through our faith in Jesus, we can see more clearly. We are no longer helpless because the word can be better understood and concrete us in our faith. We can stop tripping and stumbling through life because we can now see and see clearly to take the narrow path. Once the blinders are taken off by faith in Jesus, we can navigate through life knowing and seeing and walking in the way that we need to go.

Peter Walks on Water

After He had sent them away, He went up on the mountain by Himself to pray. When evening came, He was there alone, but the boat was already far from land, buffeted by the waves because the wind was against it.

During the fourth watch of the night, Jesus went out to them, walking on the sea. When the disciples saw Him walking on the sea, they were terrified. "It's a ghost!" they said, and cried out in fear.

But Jesus spoke up at once: "Take courage! It is I. Do not be afraid."

"Lord, if it is You," Peter replied, "command me to come to You on the water."

"Come," said Jesus.

Then Peter got down out of the boat, walked on the water, and came toward Jesus. But when he saw the strength of the wind, he was afraid, and beginning to sink, cried out, "Lord, save me!"

Immediately Jesus reached out His hand and took hold of Peter. "You of little faith," He said, "why did you doubt?" (Matthew 14:23-31)

I believe everyone knows this story, Peter walking on the water. Aside from Jesus revealing his deity to the disciples, Peter wanted to join him on the water. What did Peter do wrong? Peter took his eyes off Jesus and worried about what was going on around him. Peter was out of the boat, physically walking on the water, caught up in his thoughts and fears, and then started to sink. Could the sinking have been because of doubt, unbelief, worry, etc.? Really, no one knows but Jesus and Jesus saved Peter and wouldn't let him drown. I'm not saying to jump off a perfectly good boat or bridge into a large body of water with high winds and an incoming hurricane passing through. What I am saying is to keep your eyes on Jesus in all situations and you won't sink. Keep your eyes on Jesus always and you will never be steered wrong.

Gentile Woman's Prayers are Answered

Leaving that place, Jesus withdrew to the district of Tyre and Sidon. And a Canaanite woman from that region came to Him, crying out, "Lord, Son of David, have mercy on me! My daughter is miserably possessed by a demon."

But Jesus did not answer a word. So His disciples came and urged Him, "Send her away, for she keeps crying out after us."

He answered, "I was sent only to the lost sheep of the house of Israel."

The woman came and knelt before Him. "Lord, help me!" she said.

> *But Jesus replied, "It is not right to take the children's bread and toss it to the dogs."*
>
> *"Yes, Lord," she said, "even the dogs eat the crumbs that fall from their master's table."*
>
> *"O woman," Jesus answered, "your faith is great! Let it be done for you as you desire." And her daughter was healed from that very hour. (Matthew 15:21-28)*

A woman of Canaan came and pleaded with Jesus to save her daughter. Because of her faith, Jesus had mercy on her and saved her daughter, though she probably worshipped other gods. God has mercy on all because all people on this earth are His creation. If the people's faith is turned to Him, faith in prayer, and faith in life to follow God, He is faithful and true to come through in every and all situations. We might not realize, like, or see God's responses, but they are always for the best. To reinforce this point, below are the words of God to the prophet Ezekiel:

> *But if the wicked man turns from all the sins he has committed, keeps all My statutes, and does what is just and right, he will surely live; he will not die. None of the transgressions he has committed will be held against him. Because of the righteousness he has practiced, he will live. (Ezekiel 18:21-22)*

How is that for reassurance in the God of the Universe? If one's faith in God is established and they live for and follow him, all wrongs will be wiped clean.

Concluding Thoughts

Who better to learn about faith from, than Jesus Christ? He is our Lord and Savior. Through various examples and events, Jesus shows the importance of faith in the four gospels. Jesus also shows His compassion for all people through the text. I believe the compassion Jesus has for humanity is also the compassion of God, our heavenly Father. Their compassion means that they are ready to act on our behalf as long as it aligns with their will. If we have faith, as in the examples in this section, we would have testimony after testimony to share.

Practical Application:

We need to be fully rooted in the faith. Jesus has shown us many ways in the Scripture about how and why faith is important.

- Pray with faith that what you ask will come to pass.

- When healed/saved by faith, ALWAYS worship the one who brought you out.

  o In Exodus, the Hebrew people lost faith in God and had to wander for forty years in the wilderness versus a couple of weeks. Worshiping the one that saved you will keep you rooted in your faith.

- Faith in Jesus can help you clearly see the way that you need to go. Keeping on the straight and narrow path will keep you from wandering off track and getting stuck with someone who wasn't intended for you.

- Keep your eyes on and faith in Jesus when times get tough. Don't let the storms of life distract you and cause you to sink in your situation.

  o Faith equals flotation.

  o Faith in Jesus will always keep you afloat.

- Faith in Jesus and living for God will lead one to forgiveness of sins and a life of freedom.

CHAPTER 9

The Apostle Paul on Faith

The Apostle Paul wrote the majority of the New Testament. After he (previously named Saul of Tarsus) met Jesus on the road to Damascus after massively persecuting Christians. He was transformed to be a powerful weapon in God's arsenal. Paul studied under some of the best teachers of the Pharisees. Once Paul was saved and converted to Christianity through the power of God, his doctrine was straightened out to know the truth. Paul was then sent out to preach the gospel to the Gentiles. Let us dive into the words of Paul on faith.

First, I thank my God through Jesus Christ for all of you, because your faith is being proclaimed all over the world. (Romans 1:8)

Your faith is being proclaimed all over the world! Paul was writing this to Gentile believers in Rome. Remember, Jesus taught to all the Jewish people but had encounters with Gentiles (see previous chapter for examples, also see Matthew 15:22-29 and Matthew 8:5-13). I mention this because during the time of the New Testament, we would all be considered gentiles to Jewish people, unless you were born in a Jewish family. Now, with the truth revealed by Jesus regarding the fact that anyone can be saved, those who have not known the scriptures (everything that we call the Old Testament today), had greater faith than the Jewish people who experienced Jesus walking the earth. If we recall, they had crucified the very messiah who was sent to deliver them and the entire world from the curse of sin and death.

Be on the alert. Stand firm in the faith. Be men of courage. Be strong. (1 Corinthians 16:13)

If there was a clarion call for today, this would be it. Paul was encouraging one church that was dealing with a fine line of allowing paganism and disorder into the church (God is all about order, not about chaos). For today, we must always be on the lookout for the enemy trying to find their way into the church. Some people give up so easily instead of persevering through the trials and tribulations. "Be men of courage," we must remain steadfast in our faith and keep on the straight and narrow. I encourage everyone to grow deeper in the Lord. Allow those roots to be set in deep. Know when God is and isn't moving. Believe God will move and act by faith per what is written in the word.

Righteousness and Living by Faith

I am not ashamed of the gospel, because it is the power of God for salvation to everyone who believes, first to the Jew, then to the Greek. For the gospel reveals the righteousness of God that comes by faith from start to finish, just as it is written: "The righteous will live by faith." (Romans 1:16-17)

God offers salvation to those who believe in the death, burial, and resurrection of Jesus Christ. Through that belief, we become righteous according to our faith. Now, faith in Jesus Christ and His finished work on the cross is not something to boast proudly about. WHAT? Bear with me while I explain. We can boast in our faith out of love for the people. We can boast by sharing our testimonies with others, sharing the goodness of God. Not being boastful because "we are saved" and reminding others what's waiting for them after death, everything must come from a place of love. Sometimes a hard word has to be given to a brother or sister in the Lord, but that hard word must come from a place of love. The Lord guides us with His rod and staff. The staff is for guidance, the rod is for correction. Both are to be used out of a place of love. We are no different when interacting with others. Our heart posture always determines our location in the Lord.

Salvation by Faith

But what does it say? "The word is near you; it is in your mouth and in your heart," that is, the word of faith we are proclaiming: that if you confess with your mouth, "Jesus is Lord," and believe in your heart that God raised Him from the dead, you will be saved. For with your heart you believe and are justified, and with your mouth you confess and are saved.

It is just as the Scripture says: "Anyone who believes in Him will never be put to shame." For there is no difference between Jew and Greek: The same Lord is Lord of all, and gives richly to all who call on Him, for, "Everyone who calls on the name of the Lord will be saved." (Romans 10:8-13)

The salvation of any believer, regardless of where they are from, born, live, etc., is perfectly available to all those that follow the above scripture. The proclamation of our faith must come from our mouth, and we must believe it in our hearts. God doesn't accept lip service; He knows our heart's posture. But for those who confess and believe in their heart, they are saved.

Some people overuse the last verse in the wrong context (Everyone who calls on the name of the Lord will be saved). One can interpret that verse as "Anyone and everyone can call out to God for a get out of jail/hospital/casket free card." The great thing about our God is that He might just hear you and have mercy on you if you aren't one of His children. Our God is a God that loves His creation. He loves us so much that He gives us the choice to choose Him or this world. For those that put their trust in Him, that is true faith. One with that true faith who truly believes and proclaims their faith, God will definitely watch out for you in hard times.

Righteousness Revealed and the Law

But now, apart from the law, the righteousness of God has been revealed, as attested by the Law and the Prophets. And this righteousness from God comes through faith in Jesus Christ to all who believe. There is no distinction, for all have sinned and fall short of the glory of God, and are justified freely by His grace through the redemption that is in Christ Jesus.

God presented Him as the atoning sacrifice through faith in His blood, in order to demonstrate His righteousness, because in His forbearance He had passed over the sins committed beforehand. He did this to demonstrate His righteousness at the present time, so as to be just and to justify the one who has faith in Jesus.

Where, then, is boasting? It is excluded. On what principle? On that of works? No, but on that of faith. For we maintain that a man is justified by faith apart from works of the law.

Is God the God of Jews only? Is He not the God of Gentiles too? Yes, of Gentiles too, since there is only one God, who will justify the circumcised by faith and the uncircumcised through that same faith.

Do we, then, nullify the law by this faith? Certainly not! Instead, we uphold the law. (Romans 3:21-31)

Notice above that we have all sinned and fallen short of the glory of God. Derek Prince mentioned in one of his teachings that we are born into sin and how we unknowingly apply it. If you are a parent, remember when your children were babies? They knew naturally how to get your attention, what to do to get held, the fake crying, throwing things down to see your reaction, and the list can keep going on and on. Derek Prince points this out as manipulation. It is engrained in our nature because babies didn't learn it from their parents; we are all simply born this way.[21] This proves that we humans are naturally born with this sinful nature. I can attest that when one (parents or their friends) thinks you are a perfect child, there is more than meets the eye. I mention this not to boast, but to say that no matter how one lives or is set apart from the world, that sinful nature is there until God enters in like a flood and washes you clean and then you have to maintain it.

---

[21] *Derek Prince.*

But God presented Himself as Jesus Christ and a living sacrifice so we could be free from sin and live righteously by faith. Notice that this section of scripture reinforces the idea that boasting is excluded. Faith, apart from the works of the law, doesn't mean that Christians can live and do whatever they want to. Faith, apart from works, means that God's grace saves us if we accidentally do something wrong. Once we realize we did something wrong, we should swiftly correct ourselves.

As the last verse mentions, we uphold the law by faith, not nullify the law. Let us all rejoice that faith in Jesus saves us! We were all once sinners, have repented, and now are living by faith in our Lord and Savior Jesus Christ.

Why the Law and Works Don't Mesh

What then will we say? That the Gentiles, who did not pursue righteousness, have obtained it, a righteousness that is by faith; but Israel, who pursued a law of righteousness, has not attained it.

Why not? Because their pursuit was not by faith, but as if it were by works. They stumbled over the stumbling stone, as it is written: "See, I lay in Zion a stone of stumbling and a rock of offense;

and the one who believes in Him will never be put to shame. *(Romans 9:30-33)*

It has been mentioned earlier that Jesus came to fulfill the law, not to abolish it (see Matthew 5:17-20). In the previous sub-section, it is mentioned that righteousness was revealed through the law (see Romans 3:21-31). By the above scripture, having faith is also righteousness. During the time of the New Testament, the Jewish people who were converted to Christianity kept trying to bring back all the laws of Moses in different locations. Paul had to clear this up with the church in Rome because most of the believers there were pagans and were not familiar with Judaism. The converted pagans in Rome 100% believed in and had faith in Jesus Christ as their Lord and Savior. However, the Jewish people in Rome kept insisting on utilizing the Law of Moses, hence the correction from Paul was necessary.

The Jewish people were prophesied about in the Old Testament regarding what they would do to Jesus (see Isaiah 8:12-15 and Isaiah 28:16). They kept trying to go back to their old ways to follow the law of Moses to live righteously. All that has to be done is have faith that Jesus saved us on the cross, believe in the gospel's good news, and rest in Him. It is that simple.

Justified by Faith to Enter God's Grace

Therefore, since we have been justified through faith, we have peace with God through our Lord Jesus Christ, through whom we have gained access by faith into this grace in which we stand. And we rejoice in the hope of the glory of God. (Romans 5:1-2)

For it is by grace you have been saved through faith, and this not from yourselves; it is the gift of God, not by works, so that no one can boast. (Ephesians 2:8-9)

The Apostle Paul brings up a good point here. Since we are believers in the death, burial, and resurrection of Jesus Christ, we have faith in Jesus Christ as our Lord and Savior. Our salvation lies in His finished work on the cross. With the faith we have, God grants us the grace to live continually under His mercy. We need to remember that we don't attain this grace by mere works or by earning it. The only way to attain this wonderful gift of grace is absolute obedience to the Lord and our belief in Jesus.

Grace is such a wonderful thing. In the Old Testament, under the law of Moses, if someone broke a commandment (even a child), they were stoned to death where everyone could see and participate. Jesus showed a great measure of grace publicly with the woman caught in the very act of adultery (see John 8:1-11). Everyone was ready, with stones in hand, to kill her. When Jesus said "Let he who is without sin among you be the first to cast a stone," they all could do nothing and left. This is the grace of God. When everyone accuses you and wants nothing to do with you, God sees your heart and forgives you. The scriptures don't say it, but I believe that the woman was truly sorry and repentant in her heart. Actually, I believe she was lured into adultery because "she was caught in the very act" by the same people who wanted Jesus dead. Either way, we should thank God daily for loving us through our faults and trials. Most of us are here today by his grace and mercy.

Faith Comes by Hearing

How then can they call on the One in whom they have not believed? And how can they believe in the One of whom they have not heard? And how can they hear without someone to preach? And how can they preach unless they are sent? As it is written: "How beautiful are the feet of those who bring good news!" But not all of them welcomed the good news. For Isaiah says, "Lord, who has believed our message?" Consequently, faith comes by hearing, and hearing by the word of Christ. (Romans 10:14-17)

The Apostle Paul is once again talking about the people of Israel, not the Romans. The people of Israel had heard the gospel preached but didn't want to hear it (see Romans 10:18-21). Romans 10:21 states that God had His hands held out to "a disobedient and obstinate people." Many times in the Old Testament, God was angry with the people of Israel. They pursued after other gods and not the one that delivered them from the bondage of Egypt.

The scripture above refers to sharing the gospel and the goodness of God to others. Have you ever had your faith rise by hearing a testimony? I sure have. Paul is mentioning this very thing. Faith can come by hearing the word of God or by the testimony of believers. We are successful when declaring the goodness of God in our lives to others, both believers and non-believers. Let us allow our feet to be beautiful in the Lord's sight and be eager to share the goodness of God openly with others.

Faith Activates the Gift of Prophecy

We have different gifts according to the grace given us. If one's gift is prophecy, let him use it in proportion to his faith; (Romans 12:6)

All I have to say is WOW! If one's gift is prophecy, let him use it in proportion to his faith. How amazing is this discovery in scripture! For all the cessationists reading this book, please don't put it down. This is very important. Before the Lord drew me close, I did not know what prophecy, gifts of the spirit, or anything was. The first time I heard the word "Prophecy" was when I was a child on a Nintendo (yes, the original NES) game. I really didn't know what it meant, but I eventually figured it out. Did I know the word prophecy was in the Bible? Nope, I sure didn't. Did they really teach that when I grew up going to church? No, I don't remember one sermon about it. Here is the important part: ALL people can prophesy. Yes, I said it and it is true. People in New Age prophesy, there are prophets in false churches that claim to be Christian and much more. Prophecy can be a very wide topic to cover. For now, we will continue to discuss faith.

If one's faith is great and they have the gift of prophecy, they can prophesy much. This doesn't mean you watch a YouTube video and start walking up to strangers and go for it. Each gift needs to be nurtured and grown. Just like a baby, a pet, a plant, etc. everyone needs to grow in their gift. But the one thing that can really activate and propel the gift of prophecy and ALL other spiritual gifts is the faith that it will and can happen. If one believes it can't happen, it is the same as if they don't believe in Jesus' death on the cross. If this happens, can one have salvation in the finished work of Jesus Christ? No, because they don't believe. That is exactly how the gifts of the spirit work. If you or the entire congregation don't believe it, it just won't happen. All it takes is one person with great faith to believe in a sea of ones who don't believe, and if God wills it, it shall happen. All I am saying is, don't put God in a box. He parted the entire Red Sea and made the sea bed completely dry for the Hebrews to cross during the Exodus from Egypt. Since He is the same yesterday, today, and forever, do you think His power isn't available now? If you put God in a box, a box you shall receive.

No Judgement Zone to the Weak

Accept him whose faith is weak, without passing judgment on his opinions. For one person has faith to eat all things, while another, who is weak, eats only vegetables. The one who eats everything must not belittle the one who does not, and the one who does not eat everything must not judge the one who does, for God has accepted him. Who are you to judge someone else's servant? To his own master he stands or falls. And he will stand, for the Lord is able to make him stand. (Romans 14:1-4)

We should not judge our fellow brothers and sisters in the faith. Doesn't this sound like something Jesus taught during the Sermon on the Mount? Yes, but the Apostle Paul goes a little deeper. In Israel, during the time of the first-century church, people still adhered to the Jewish dietary laws and restrictions. Matter of fact; some people still do today. I won't dive into the subject of eating, but we are free to eat whatever we wish because Jesus even said:

"Do you not yet realize that whatever enters the mouth goes into the stomach and then is eliminated? But the things that come out of the mouth come from the heart, and these things defile a man. For out of the heart come evil thoughts, murder, adultery, sexual immorality, theft, false testimony, and slander. These are

what defile a man, but eating with unwashed hands does not defile him." (Matthew 15:17-20)

These two sections of scripture mirror each other. It is okay if someone is doing something you don't do. We all have different walks with the Lord. We all aren't robots coming off the end of an assembly line. If we all dressed the same, ate the same food, said the same exact words as answers to the same questions, etc., we would either be robots or in a cult. The bottom line is if someone feels compelled to be a vegan and not bathe but loves God with all their heart, the person who takes three showers a day and eats junk food and nothing but meat all day that also loves God with all their heart shouldn't say anything about one another. We are all brothers and sisters; we shouldn't quarrel or cause strife. Look at your own family. Is it perfect, and no one does anything wrong? There isn't that weird uncle, aunt, or cousin all the others talk about? Per the words of Jesus and the Apostle Paul above, we should not judge but love them all. Even if we disagree or if they crossed us a time or two, keep on loving and don't defile yourself by speaking anything that wouldn't be edifying or bring glory to God.

Faith without Love is Dead

If I have the gift of prophecy and can fathom all mysteries and all knowledge, and if I have absolute faith so as to move mountains, but have not love, I am nothing. (1 Corinthians 13:2)

But by faith we eagerly await through the Spirit the hope of righteousness. For in Christ Jesus neither circumcision nor uncircumcision has any value. All that matters is faith, expressed through love. (Galatians 5:5-6)

I touched on this in the previous scripture. The above two scriptures further solidify the fact that, without love, nothing has any worth. I am reminded of King Solomon stating:

I have seen all the works which have been done under the sun, and behold, all is vanity, a futile grasping and chasing after the wind. What is crooked cannot be straightened and what is defective and lacking cannot be counted. (Ecclesiastes 1:14-15 AMP)

How does this correlate? Well, love is not vanity and chasing after the wind. Chasing after the wind is the gifts, riches, wealth, fame, status, etc. basically anything that can glorify one's self. Let us be ones that love one another. If we don't, wouldn't we be considered crooked and defective? What does King Solomon say about what happens to something crooked or defective? That is right, it cannot be straightened and it cannot be counted. Wouldn't that put that type of person in the place of a sinner? Yes, it most definitely would. Uh oh, are we not supposed to examine ourselves and watch what we do and speak? Of course! We are to be self-disciplined. We are to watch what we say and do, for our words and actions can speak of our own character. Since we are ambassadors of Christ, let us set a great example through self-discipline and love one another unconditionally.

Faith Creates Obedience

Now to Him who is able to strengthen you by my gospel and by the proclamation of Jesus Christ, according to the revelation of the mystery concealed for ages past but now revealed and made known through the writings of the prophets by the command of the eternal God, in order to lead all nations to the obedience that comes from faith to the only wise God be glory forever through Jesus Christ! Amen. (Romans 16:25-27)

Some people might call this loyalty. I would say yes and no. No, because one can be loyal to someone or something but have absolutely zero trust in that person or thing. That is not true faith then, is it? Faith in the finished work of the cross creates in us obedience (and in turn loyalty) to God.

Faith over time in God is like a brick or Lego piece. The greater the length of time one's faith is in the Lord, the larger the brick wall or Lego project becomes. Our goal is to be a complete castle or Lego city. The more that is built as a whole, the greater the obedience to God, which is our ultimate goal. God is a king; a king is sovereign. If we are followers and He is our king, we must obey His commands or suffer the consequences. This might sound a little harsh, but even princes and princesses have to obey the king. The point is, we need to always be obedient to His call and what He wants us to do. The obedience generated by our faith in Him will continue to grow more and more as time goes on.

Faith in Christ is a Son of Abraham

So also, "Abraham believed God, and it was credited to him as righteousness." Understand, then, that those who have faith are sons of Abraham. The Scripture foresaw that God would justify the Gentiles by faith, and foretold the gospel to Abraham: "All nations will be blessed through you." So those who have faith are blessed along with Abraham, the man of faith. (Galatians 3:6-9)

All those who walk by faith are true sons of Abraham. In Chapter 8 of the Gospel of John, Jesus was speaking to the Pharisees who were plotting to kill Him; Jesus was explaining how the truth will set you free and that whoever sins is a slave to sin. The Pharisees got their feelings hurt because they didn't understand Jesus' teaching.

"Abraham is our father," they (Pharisees) replied. "If you were children of Abraham," said Jesus, "you would do the works of Abraham." (John 8:39)

To cut out the extra verses, Jesus explained Abraham walked as a son and not as an enslaved person. Yes, Abraham had his downfalls, just like everyone, but he learned from those mistakes. The one major factor for Abraham being the father of many nations wasn't his wealth, power, family lineage, etc.; it was his faith. If it weren't for Abraham's faith, God would have used someone else. Without Abraham's faith, he wouldn't have been credited as righteous in the eyes of God (see Genesis 15:6 and Romans 4:3). Without Abraham's righteousness (ultimately his faith in God), we could not live freely because of his blessing. You see, if we still lived under the law of Moses, we would be slaves. Since we are set free from Jesus' finished work on the cross, we get to rest in the blessing of Abraham. God revealed what was to happen in the future, and Abraham knew of the coming messiah.

"Your father Abraham rejoiced that he would see My day. He saw it and was glad." (John 8:56)

Why did Abraham rejoice? Abraham knew he lived in a fallen world; it was all around him his entire life. Abraham knew that the coming messiah would break the chains of sin and death once and for all. That is why he was glad; through him the entire world would be set free. Let us keep walking as sons in the blessing of Abraham and not slaves to sin.

Faith Removes Us from the Curse of the Law

All who rely on works of the law are under a curse. For it is written: "Cursed is everyone who does not continue to do everything written in the Book of the Law." Now it is clear that no one is justified before God by the law, because, "The righteous will live by faith." The law, however, is not based on faith; on the contrary, "The man who does these things will live by them."

Christ redeemed us from the curse of the law by becoming a curse for us. For it is written: "Cursed is everyone who is hung on a tree." He redeemed us in order that the blessing promised to Abraham would come to the Gentiles in Christ Jesus, so that by faith we might receive the promise of the Spirit. (Galatians 3:10-14)

Sometimes, the Apostle Paul's writings are a little hard to follow. The above scripture is an extension of what has already been mentioned. We have already mentioned that whoever lives under the law is a slave. The above mentions that if one lives under the law, they are cursed. Curses are as real today as they were back then. Since righteous people live by faith (through the blessing of Abraham), we are no longer under the law. How is this so? Since Jesus made himself a curse when crucified (on a cross, the cross is a tree since it was made of wood), supernaturally, he took the curse from us forever. Salvation at its finest, the finished work of Jesus Christ on the cross. If it isn't apparent by now, this is why Christians say Jesus is our savior. Everyone in the entire world is saved from the power of sin and death (spiritual death and damnation to hell) if desired. All that has to be done is the belief that Jesus died for our sins, and rose again on the third day and later ascended to heaven. Walking in faith, knowing that Jesus is our Lord and Savior, removes us from the law of Moses.

Can Access God's Presence Through Faith

In Him and through faith in Him we may enter God's presence with boldness and confidence. (Ephesians 3:12)

YES PLEASE!!! If God's presence were on a buffet, no other dish would need to be served. To keep this verse in the proper context, the Apostle Paul explains that through Jesus, even Gentiles can access the presence of God. The common theme after the four gospels is this very concept. Salvation is for all humanity. The one thing that keeps ringing in my spirit is the application of prayer and this verse. We have mentioned before the classic verse of having faith the size of a mustard seed will move mountains (which is directly applied through prayer). In prayer, we indeed have access to God's presence. The access is all granted through faith in Jesus. It might sound complicated, but it truly is not. If we follow the basic format of prayer that Jesus gave us (Our Father, who art in heaven....) and continue to press in (don't just repeat the scripture but use it as a template for prayer). God's tangible presence is tangible and available during prayer. When in the presence of God, I don't want to leave. And even if God's tangible presence doesn't happen during prayer, He still hears the prayers of those who earnestly seek Him.

Faith is a Shield

In addition to all this, take up the shield of faith, with which you can extinguish all the flaming arrows of the evil one. (Ephesians 6:16)

Everyone should be well accustomed to the spiritual armor listed in Ephesians Chapter 6. Let us chew on this scripture a bit. Shield of faith, what does a shield do? Well, its primary use is to defend the person holding it. Regarding defense, per scripture, faith will extinguish the "flaming arrows of the evil one." What are flaming arrows? Statements such as "You are never good enough to serve God, just give up," or "It is okay to smoke that, no one is looking," or "Man, they are handsome (or beautiful), no one will know about this," and the list can go on and on. Flaming arrows are basically any temptation of the enemy. Remember what we have discussed: faith leads to obedience, obedience in God's ways. We are to die to our fleshly and soulish desires daily. Resist all the temptations of the enemy to be successful in our walk.

Submit yourselves, then, to God. Resist the devil, and he will flee from you. (James 4:7)

Our best offense is our defense. Satan, we do not want anything from you! Not today, yesterday, or tomorrow, so put that in your pipe and smoke it!

Concluding Thoughts

As mentioned above, "Faith" is mentioned in the New Testament almost 250 times. The above explanations of portions of scripture should help highlight some keys from the scriptures. I encourage all to dig into the scriptures more. I did not even get into the rest of the New Testament Letters, focusing solely on Jesus and Paul. Something not emphasized is the people's faith Paul ministered to. Christians were under heavy persecution; many were martyred for their faith in Jesus Christ. Christians in the first-century church had to lift each other up. There was not a church on every other street corner then. The believers lived and congregated in a general area (think of a state, province, city, and all surrounding small towns as general areas). Why mention all of this? All the keys mentioned above rooted them in their faith to persevere through all the hard times and persecution. The same goes for modern-day believers. Faith is the fuel that keeps us alive in Christ.

Practical Application:

The Apostle Paul expounded on more topics than Jesus, all equally important. Remember, during the time of Paul, many churches and believers were being persecuted.

- We all have a call to be courageous, steadfast, and strong in the faith.

- Always put your trust and faith in Jesus. That is the basis of our salvation and righteousness.

- We are all born sinners with a sinful nature.
    - Christians can't strive for salvation by our works.
    - We only have salvation by faith in the finished work of Jesus' death on the cross.

- Believers live under the blessing of Abraham, living by faith. If we stumble, the grace of God saves us.

- We must share the gospel and our testimonies to raise the faith of others.

- Our level of faith determines our level of operation in the gift of prophecy.

- Do not put God in a box!

- Don't judge a brother or sister. We should love them unconditionally, no matter what their shortcomings might be.

- God's presence is accessed by our faith in and through Jesus and is attainable through prayer.

- Our faith is a shield against the enemy's attacks.

Conclusion

The composition of this book has truly been an adventure. Much has been learned through the process. I pray the items covered and explained through this volume have been a blessing to its readers. Remaining in the middle versus the Left or Right side of everything was difficult, but I believe that balance is needed to remain properly grounded in the faith. I pray that parts of, if not all, of this book have been a blessing.

We have gone on quite the journey of covering many topics, ranging from:

- The beginning of time and the creation of the earth
- The significance of the Fall of Man

- God's laws that have been established:
  - Physical Laws like Gravity
  - Mathematics
  - Physical and Spiritual Realms
  - Relation of time and distance in each realm
- God's Kingdom on Earth
  - Garden of Eden
  - The Great Flood
  - Abraham's Blessing
- Old Covenant (Ten Commandments)
- New Covenant (Jesus' Sermon on the Mount)
- Jesus and the Apostle Paul's teachings and written accounts of faith

Through all the content covered, the focus of everything revolving around Christianity is Jesus and His finished work on the cross. Always remember that love is the most important thing. Per the Apostle Paul, without love, we are nothing (see 1 Corinthians 13:2). Per Jesus, all will know we are His disciples from our love for one another (including Christians and non-Christians alike) (see John 13:35). Our heart posture should also be centered on the love of the Father. We are all God's children. It is ultimately up to us to draw near to

Him or choose not to. God loves us so much; we get a choice to choose Him. If you have made it all the way through this book and you don't personally know or haven't given God your 100% yes, and you would like to. Please turn to the next section to be led through the Prayer of Salvation.

Prayer of Salvation

All your life, God has loved you. He knows you intimately and thoroughly. He has numbered the hairs on your head and keeps your tears in a bottle. Today, He wants to write your name in the Book of Life. In fact, God loves you so much that He sent His Son, Jesus, to die for your sins so that you could have an abundant and eternal life. If you want to be saved from your sins and have a personal relationship with the God who created you and loved you enough to die for you, pray this simple prayer with sincerity from your heart:

Dear God,

I acknowledge that Jesus Christ is Your Son. I believe that He was born of a virgin. He died on the cross and shed His blood for my sins. He arose from the dead, and He is seated at Your right hand interceding for me. I confess that I AM A SINNER and have disobeyed Your commandments.

I ask You to forgive me of my sins because of the blood of Jesus and not because of any good that I have done. I ask You, Lord Jesus, to come into my heart and be my Savior and Lord. Place my name in Your Book and put Your Spirit within me so I can live for You.

I confess with my mouth and believe in my heart that I AM BORN AGAIN. Thank You, Father, in Jesus' name, I pray. Amen.

If you pray this prayer and truly believe the words spoken, you have accepted the Holy Spirit to come and dwell within you (this is the start of the process called "Regeneration"). Support your decision to have a personal relationship with Jesus by spending time in prayer, reading the Bible, attending a Bible teaching church (can be a home church, small group, or Bible Study), and getting water baptized. I believe in being baptized in the Holy Spirit; some do not. Everyone has a unique experience with Holy Spirit Baptisms. As mentioned in my testimony, one can pray to receive it just as I did (no one has to pray over you). I also recommend Inner Healing when one is comfortable. The most important thing to remember is God wants a relationship with us as His children. That relationship needs to be nurtured above anything else.

This section was adapted from:
https://www.rhfan.com/prayer-of-salvation/

References

BIBLE REFERENCES:
AMP (Amplified Bible): accessed via biblegateway.com
BSB (Berean Standard Bible): accessed via
    bereanbible.com

BIBLIOGRAPHY:
Bernis, Jonathan. "How Many Messianic Prophecies Did
    Jesus Fulfill in Scripture?" FIRM Israel, January 31,
    2015. https://firmisrael.org/learn/how-many-
    messianic-prophecies-did-jesus-fulfill/.
Britannica.com Encyclopædia. "How Did St. Peter Die? |
    Britannica." Accessed September 15, 2024.
    https://www.britannica.com/question/How-did-
    St-Peter-die.
Britannica.com Encyclopædia. "Saint John the Apostle |
    Biography, Facts, Feast Day, Writings, & Death |
    Britannica," July 22, 2024.
    https://www.britannica.com/biography/Saint-
    John-the-Apostle.
Derek Prince: The Nature of Witchcraft, 2014.
    https://www.youtube.com/watch?v=C23uxjUZLH
    A.
Duval, Daniel. *Higher Dimensions, Parallel Dimensions,
    and the Spirit Realm*. BookBaby, 2016.
Mark, Joshua J. "Ur." World History Encyclopedia.
    Accessed October 13, 2024.
    https://www.worldhistory.org/ur/.
Merriam-Webster.com Dictionary. "Definition of COVET,"
    September 5, 2024. https://www.merriam-
    webster.com/dictionary/covet.
Merriam-Webster.com Dictionary. "Definition of
    CREATIONISM." Accessed July 28, 2024.

https://www.merriam-webster.com/dictionary/creationism.

Merriam-Webster.com Dictionary. "Definition of FAITH," August 25, 2024. https://www.merriam-webster.com/dictionary/faith.

Merriam-Webster.com Dictionary. "Definition of HYPOTHESIS," July 29, 2024. https://www.merriam-webster.com/dictionary/hypothesis.

Merriam-Webster.com Dictionary. "Definition of SANHEDRIN." Accessed September 19, 2024. https://www.merriam-webster.com/dictionary/Sanhedrin.

Merriam-Webster.com Dictionary. "Definition of SATURDAY," September 4, 2024. https://www.merriam-webster.com/dictionary/Saturday.

Merriam-Webster.com Dictionary. "Definition of SCIENCE," July 30, 2024. https://www.merriam-webster.com/dictionary/science.

Merriam-Webster.com Dictionary. "Definition of THEORY," August 2, 2024. https://www.merriam-webster.com/dictionary/theory.

Nakoa, Thierry. *The Testimony of Jesus-Is the Spirit of Prophecy: School of the Holy Spirit Manual 3a.* Thierry Nakoa, 2024.

Rennie, John. "15 Answers to Creationist Nonsense." Scientific American, July 1, 2002. https://www.scientificamerican.com/article/15-answers-to-creationist/.

Strong, James. *The New Strong's Expanded Exhaustive Concordance of the Bible.* Expanded edition. Thomas Nelson, 2010.

Torrey, R. A. *How to Obtain Fullness of Power.* Whitaker House, 1982.

Author's Biography

Terry J. Goble is an engineer, husband, father, and faithful disciple of Jesus Christ. Many would call him brother or friend, always being patient, kind, and willing to share and show the heart of the father to those who do and don't know the Lord. Terry walks in love, humility, and compassion for the world while operating in the Spirit of the Fear of the Lord and humbleness. He is passionate about sharing the truth of the Gospel, helping the less fortunate, and being led by the Holy Spirit while living as a priest and king in the order of Melchizedek. Terry is being led into his calling by the Lord through the gifts of the Spirit and is continually learning each day. Terry appreciates his family and others that are also walking with him on this journey.

In his spare time, Terry likes to enjoy nature, camping, reading, spending time with friends and family, home improvement, mechanics, and more. Terry humbly allows the Lord to lead him and his family through whatever the world throws at them. He has been blessed with a faithful wife and three wonderful children that are all in love with and willing to serve the Lord.

Author's Testimony

Since many might not know who I am, I included a little about myself and my testimony. I grew up in a small Midwest farming community in America. Only two churches were in town, and the running joke was always which one was better. I have been on a longer walk with God than I'd like to admit. Sadly, I was not aware of this until I was in my late thirties. I feel the Lord has been working on me since I was a youth. Maybe you feel the same? When I was close to graduating High School at seventeen, something happened at the church we attended while I was going through confirmation. What happened turned me away from God for a long time. Should it have bothered me? Probably not, but other factors came into play, and I left the church. Since High School, I became quite the enabler to others, and I continued to perfect that craft as time passed. My college years were full of drinking, partying, things I really shouldn't have been doing, and leading other people away from God (basically living for the world). I wouldn't listen to any of the Christians at college. My friends and I made fun of them even though I knew there was some truth to it. I thought living in the world was the way to go. I considered myself agnostic. I believed in a higher power because I knew there was and is one (I didn't realize it was the God [Jehovah, Yahweh, YHWH] of the Bible). For this reason, I couldn't go full blown as an atheist because of childhood experiences, though I was being pulled that way by some. I just couldn't do it.

Moving into post-college life, nothing much changed. I simultaneously turned into a functioning alcoholic, and borderline narcoleptic, among many other things I'm not too proud of. At that place, it got really lonely. When I originally thought life was going to be one constant party to the next, my life was actually spiraling downhill and fast. What I didn't realize at the time was convictions by the Holy Spirit that made me question where I was in life. I wanted to change my lifestyle, but the mess I lived in kept me stuck in quicksand. Then, I met my wife. We have a funny story, but that will be saved for another time. I thank God for her. She is the main reason I cleaned myself up.

During our early years of marriage, we went to church off and on, but no edification came from it (it was like the church I grew up in, dry and religious). We stopped going. Over the years, many trials and the blindness of not knowing that God was moving and working in our lives went unnoticed (but the trials and tribulations were evident). We, as a family, went all in for God and started a Jesus Journey.

I was pretty religious and rigid, had bad theology, went off of what others said, and hardly cracked a Bible open for over 10 minutes at a time (if I could stay awake).

Then, in March 2022, I had a random baptism of the Holy Spirit experience that changed my life forever (no matter where you are in life, God will meet you where you are). Since then, I have been hungry for more and more of God. The learning curve was pretty steep. My eyes have been opened to how much deception is out there. Trying to see/find the truth is hard. I read many books and studied the Bible, and I still felt like I had more questions than answers. Truly, I realized how fascinating Christianity was once you fully dive into it. My walk has been filled with many difficulties and God is still working on me, just like everyone else. If this is you too, just yield to the process. Yielding is better than tribulations and disobedience.

A few brothers and sisters I have met along the way have led me to know of different Christian authors and leaders. My library includes works from R. A. Torrey, E.M. Bounds, Andrew Murray, Watchman Nee, Derek Prince, and many other classic and newer authors.

Since joining the School of the Holy Spirit Church in early 2024, my Christian Walk has gone into hyper-drive. I am learning and growing in my gifts and God is and has been really moving in my life. I'm extremely thankful to be a part of a great company of individuals who live and breathe everything regarding Jesus daily.

I have a passion for helping others reach their full potential in their walk and calling. James 2:14-26 should give a wake-up call to all the lukewarm Christians out there. Let us not be like the church of Laodicea in Revelation Chapter 3. We all must come together on one accord and start affecting the world instead of picking each other apart. If the enemy can keep us divided, how can we stand as one body?

The School of the Holy Spirit

---

8 Commitments for being a Spiritual Warrior

1. **Being a Royal Priest**
   - **Prioritize** the first commandment: **Love the Lord** with all your heart, soul, and strength. Then, follow the second commandment: **love yourself** first then **love others.**
   - Priests prioritize <u>safeguarding the Lord's presence</u> in their earthly tabernacle (body and soul) first, then ministering in the heavenly tabernacle (seated in the heavenly places (spirit)).
   - **Pray Daily** (especially contemplative prayer), Dedicate at least 2 ½ hours a day to prayer.

2. **Cultivate a lifestyle of obedience and worship, rooted in the fear of the Lord.** Make it a daily practice to worship, obey, and read the Word, specifically the Book of Revelation. Fellowship with other believers.
   O worship the LORD in the beauty of holiness: fear before him, all the earth. —Psalms 96:9

3. **Consecrate and be thankful (Fasted Lifestyle).** Regal Priests consecrate themselves in their earthly tabernacle, their bodies, as their daily living sacrifices (per Psalm 24 "ascend") and (per Psalm 15 "dwell") in the heavenly tabernacle. Being Living Stones; Building a Spiritual House; Offer Spiritual Sacrifices of Righteousness; Sacrifices of Trust; Renewing your Mind (1 Peter 2:5, Psalms 4:5).

4. **Pure religion and undefiled before God:** Embrace the responsibility of being a good citizen on Earth by helping the poor, the widows, and the orphans, and lay low (James 1:27).

5. **Honor, Serve and Give extravagantly:** Give to support the kingdom by sowing into those who have paved the way for you.
   - Give elders double honor. Priest offer gifts and sacrifices to the Lord and the people (*1 Timothy 5:17*). Support your spiritual leaders with your resources and service.

6. **Make Disciples:** Duplicate yourself and give everything you have to receive more (Matthew 28:19).

7. **Power Evangelism:** He sent them to preach the kingdom of God and to heal the sick (Luke 9:2).
   - Cleanse the lepers, raise the dead, cast out demons. Prophesy and Win souls.

8. **Lead: Royal Priests Teach & Judge, Sanctify** and act as **ambassadors of His forgiveness**.
   - Preach the Gospel of the Kingdom by Teaching, Prophesying, Healing the Sick, Raising the dead. Casting out demons. Release SOZO (Greek for Saved, Healed, and Delivered) .

Figure 2: SOHS Eight Commitments of a Spiritual Warrior[22]

---

[22] Nakoa, *The Testimony of Jesus-Is the Spirit of Prophecy.*

The School of the Holy Spirit

For more information on the School of the Holy Spirit, please use the QR Code below or access the website: www.schooloftheholyspirit.church

Permissions and Inquiries

Contact tgoble.books@gmail.com with comments, inquiries, or feedback, including any permission or endorsement requests for this volume.

www.ingramcontent.com/pod-product-compliance
Lightning Source LLC
Chambersburg PA
CBHW071727120626
46550CB00002B/421